SECRETS
of the
LOST MODE
of
PRAYER

*Let yourself be
silently drawn by the
stronger pull of what
you really love.*

— Rumi

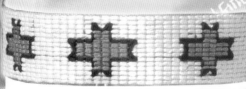

Also by Gregg Braden

Books

Deep Truth
The Divine Matrix
Fractal Time
The God Code
*The Isaiah Effect**
The Spontaneous Healing of Belief
*Walking Between the Worlds**
*Awakening to Zero Point**

Audio/CD Programs

Unleashing the Power of the God Code
The Divine Name (with Jonathan Goldman)
An Ancient Magical Prayer
(with Deepak Chopra)
Speaking the Lost Language of God
Awakening the Power of a Modern God
*The Gregg Braden Audio Collection**

*All the above are available from Hay House
except items marked with an asterisk

Please visit Hay House USA: www.hayhouse.com®
Hay House Australia: www.hayhouse.com.au
Hay House UK: www.hayhouse.co.uk
Hay House South Africa: www.hayhouse.co.za
Hay House India: www.hayhouse.co.in

SECRETS
of the
LOST MODE
of
PRAYER

The Hidden Power of Beauty, Blessing, Wisdom, and Hurt

GREGG BRADEN

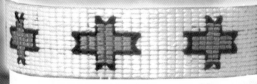

HAY HOUSE, INC.
Carlsbad, California • New York City
London • Sydney • Johannesburg
Vancouver • Hong Kong • New Delhi

Published and distributed in the United States by: Hay House, Inc.: www.hayhouse.com • *Published and distributed in Australia by:* Hay House Australia Pty. Ltd.: www.hayhouse.com.au • *Published and distributed in the United Kingdom by:* Hay House UK, Ltd.: www.hayhouse.co.uk • *Published and distributed in the Republic of South Africa by:* Hay House SA (Pty), Ltd.: www.hayhouse.co.za • *Distributed in Canada by:* Raincoast: www.raincoast.com • *Published in India by:* Hay House Publishers India: www.hayhouse.co.in

Editorial supervision: Jill Kramer
Cover and interior design: Amy Rose Grigoriou
Interior photos/illustrations: Gregg Braden and **www.photos.com**

Poem translations by Coleman Barks and others

Library of Congress Control Number: 2005920092

ISBN 13: 978-1-4019-0683-2
ISBN 10: 1-4019-0683-4

15 14 13 12   7 6 5 4
1st printing, January 2006
4th printing, April 2012

Printed in China

This book is written for those who search for comfort in the presence of fear and uncertainty in our world. In those moments when life's hurts tear into the hidden places of your soul, I invite you to enter the refuge of beauty, blessing, our lost mode of prayer, and the deep wisdom that each rests upon. It is here that you may find meaning in the unexplained, and the strength that guides you to the close of another day.

Contents

Introduction

"THERE ARE BEAUTIFUL AND WILD FORCES WITHIN US."

WITH THESE WORDS, ST. FRANCIS OF ASSISI DESCRIBED THE MYSTERY AND POWER THAT LIVES WITHIN EVERY MAN, WOMAN, AND CHILD BORN INTO THIS WORLD. THE SUFI POET RUMI FURTHER DESCRIBED THE MAGNITUDE OF THAT POWER BY COMPARING IT TO A GREAT OAR THAT PROPELS US THROUGH LIFE. "IF YOU PUT YOUR SOUL AGAINST THIS OAR WITH ME," HE BEGINS, "THE POWER THAT MADE THE UNIVERSE WILL ENTER YOUR SINEW FROM A SOURCE *NOT OUTSIDE* YOUR LIMBS, BUT FROM A HOLY REALM *THAT LIVES IN US.*"[1]

Through the language of poetry, both Rumi and St. Francis express something beyond the obvious experience of our everyday world. In the words of their times, they remind us of what the ancients called the greatest force in the universe—the power that unites us with the cosmos. Today, we know that power as "prayer." Elaborating on prayer, St. Francis simply stated, "The result of prayer is life." Prayer brings us life, he says, because it "irrigates the earth and the heart."

The Bridge to Our Past

Knowledge is the bridge that connects us with everyone who has ever lived before us. From civilization to civilization and lifetime to lifetime, we contribute the individual stories that become our collective history. No matter how well we preserve the information of the past, however, the words of these stories are little more than "data" until we give them meaning. It's the way we apply what we know of our past that becomes the wisdom of the present.

For thousands of years, for example, those who have come before us preserved the knowledge of prayer, why it works, and how we may use it in our lives. In massive temples and hidden tombs, through language and customs that have changed very little for at least 5,000 years, our ancestors preserved the powerful knowledge of prayer. The secret, however, is not found in the words of the prayers themselves. Just as the power of a computer program is more than the language in which it's written, we must search deeper to know the true power that awaits us when we pray.

It may be precisely this power that mystic George Gurdjieff discovered as the result of his lifelong search for truth. After years of following ancient clues that led him from temple to village and teacher to teacher, he found himself in a secret monastery hidden in the mountains of the Middle East. There, a great master offered the words of encouragement that made his search worthwhile: "You have now found the conditions in which the desire of your heart can become the reality of your being." I can't help but believe that prayer is part of the conditions that Gurdjieff discovered.

To unleash what St. Francis called the "beautiful and wild forces" within us and find the conditions in which our heart's desire becomes reality, we must understand our relationship to ourselves, our world, and God. Through the words of our past, we're given the knowledge of how to do just that. In his book *The Prophet,* Kahlil Gibran reminds us that we can't be taught things we already know. "No man can reveal to you," he states, "that which already lies half asleep in the dawning of your knowledge." It makes tremendous sense that hidden within us we would already have the power to communicate with the force that's responsible for our existence! To do so, however, we must discover who we *really* are.

The Two Universal Questions

The pioneering anthropologist Louis Leakey was once asked why his work to find the oldest evidence of human existence was so important. He replied, "Without an understanding of who we are, and from where we came, I do not think we can truly advance." I believe there's a lot of truth to what Leakey said—so much so that the bulk of my adult life has revolved around my search to know who we are, and how the knowledge of our past can help us become better people and create a better world.

With the exception of Antarctica, my research into the mystery of our past has taken me to every continent on the planet. From huge cities such as Cairo and Bangkok, to remote villages in Peru and Bolivia, from ancient monasteries in the Himalayas of Tibet, to Hindu temples in Nepal, during the time that I've experienced each culture, a single theme has emerged. The people of this world are ready for something more than the suffering and uncertainty that defined their lives for so much of the 20th century. They're ready for peace, and the promise of a better tomorrow.

As different as our cultures and ways of life appear on the outside, beneath the surface we're all searching for the same things—a land to call home, a way to provide for our families, and a better future for ourselves and our children. At the same time, there are two questions that people of all cultures ask me again and again, either directly or through translators. The first is simply: "What is happening to our world?"

The second is: "What can we do to make things better?" The answers to both questions appear to be woven into a single understanding that links the traditions of prayer today with the most ancient and cherished spiritual traditions of our past.

Four hundred years ago in the high deserts of the American Southwest, the great wisdom keepers of the Navajo families were tested by the earth, nature, and the tribes that surrounded them. Through the extremes that drought, intense heat, and lack of food caused in their societies, the Navajo realized that they must harness the power of their *inner* pain to endure the harsh conditions of their *outer* world. Their very survival depended upon learning to do so.

Recognizing that life's tests pushed them to the depths of their greatest suffering, they also discovered that the same tests revealed their greatest strengths. The key to their survival was to immerse themselves in life's challenges without becoming lost in the experience. They had to find an "anchor" within themselves—a belief that gave them the inner strength to endure their tests—and the knowledge that a better day would follow. From this place of power they had the confidence to take risks, change their lives, and make sense of their world.

Our lives today may not be so very different from that of those brave individuals who roamed the high deserts of the American Southwest centuries before our country was created. Although the scenery has shifted and the circumstances have changed, we still find ourselves in situations that shake the foundation of our beliefs, test the limits of our sensibilities, and challenge us to rise above the things that hurt us. In a world that many describe as "coming apart at the seams," punctuated by senseless acts of hate, record numbers of failed relationships, broken homes, and conditions that threaten the survival of entire societies, we're challenged to find a way to live each day with peace, joy, and a sense of order.

With an eloquence that's typical of such ancient wisdom, Navajo tradition describes a way of looking at life that places responsibility for our happiness or suffering squarely upon our shoulders. Preserved as the Beauty Prayer, the exact wording varies from record to record and telling to telling, although the essence of the prayer may be shared in three brief phrases. Through only 20 words, the Navajo elders convey sophisticated wisdom, reminding us of the connection between our inner and outer worlds that has been recognized only recently by modern science.

Arranged as three parts, each phrase offers insight into our power to shift the chemistry of our bodies and influence the quantum possibilities of our world. In its simplest form, the words of the prayer speak for themselves. The Navajo say, "Nizhonigoo bil iina," words that roughly translate into:

> *The beauty that you live with,*
> *The beauty that you live by,*
> *The beauty upon which you base your life.*[2]

Through the words of an author forgotten long ago, the simplicity of this prayer offers renewed hope when all else seems to have failed. But the Beauty Prayer is more than words alone. Within its simplicity lies the key to solving one of humankind's greatest mysteries: How do we survive life's hurts? Rather than playing it safe and shying away from the very situations that give meaning to each day, the power of beauty and prayer allows us to jump right into our experience, knowing that any hurt we may suffer is temporary. Through the Beauty Prayer, the Navajo people have long found strength, comfort, and a way to deal with the suffering of our world.

What secrets have traditions like those of the Navajo of the American Southwest, the monks and nuns of Tibet, and others kept safe while much of the world has strayed from our relationship to the earth, one another, and a greater power? What wisdom did they know in their time that may help us become better people, and create a better world, in ours?

Hurt, Blessing, Beauty, and Prayer

Hidden in the knowledge of those who have come before us, we find the wisdom to empower our prayers of healing and peace. From the ancient writings of the Gnostics and Essenes, to the native traditions throughout the Americas, hurt, blessing, and beauty are acknowledged as the keys to surviving our greatest tests. Prayer is the language that allows us to apply the lessons of our experiences to the situations in our lives.

From this perspective, "wisdom" and "hurt" are two extremes of the same experience. They are the beginning and completion of the same cycle. Hurt is our initial feeling, our gut response to loss, disappointment, or the news of something that shocks our emotions. Wisdom is the healed expression of our hurt. We change hurt into wisdom by finding new meaning in painful experiences. Blessing, beauty, and prayer are the tools for our change.

Twentieth-century Christian visionary Reverend Samuel Shoemaker described the power of prayer to create change in a single, poetic, and perhaps deceptively simple sentence: "Prayer may not change things for *you*," he says, "but it for sure *changes you* for things." While we may not be able to go back in time to undo the reason we hurt to begin with, we do have the power to change what the loss of loved ones, the shock of broken promises, and life's disappointments mean to us. In doing so, we open the door to move toward a healing resolution of even our most hurtful memories.

Without understanding the relationship between wisdom and hurt, our endurance of pain may seem senseless—even cruel—and continue, as the pain cycle remains open-ended. But how are we to remove ourselves from life's hurt long enough to find the wisdom in our experiences? When we're reeling from a loss, a violated trust, or a betrayal that was unthinkable only hours or moments before, how are we to find refuge from our emotions long enough to feel something else? This is where the power of blessing comes in.

Blessing Is the Release

"Blessing" is the ancient secret that releases us from life's hurt long enough to replace it with another feeling. When we bless the people or things that have hurt us, we're temporarily suspending the cycle of pain. Whether this suspension lasts for a nanosecond or an entire day makes no difference. Whatever the period of time, during the blessing a doorway opens for us to begin our healing and move on with life. The key is that for some period of time, we're released from our hurt long enough to let something else into our hearts and minds. That something is the power of "beauty."

Beauty Is the Transformer

The most sacred and ancient traditions remind us that beauty exists in all things, regardless of how we interpret them in our daily lives. Beauty is already created, and always present. While we may modify our surroundings, create new relationships, and move to new locations to please our ever-changing ideas of balance and harmony, the building blocks that go into such beauty are already there.

Beyond an appreciation for the things that are simply pleasing to our eyes, beauty is described by wisdom traditions as an *experience* that also touches our hearts, minds, and souls. Through our ability to perceive beauty in even the "ugliest" moments of life, we may elevate ourselves long enough to give new meaning to our hurt. In this way, beauty is a trigger that launches us into a new perspective. The key, however, is that it appears to be dormant until we give it our attention. Beauty awakens only when we invite it into our lives.

Our Lost Mode of Prayer

We find ourselves in a world of experiences that defy our sensibilities and push us to the limits of what we can accept as rational, loving people. In the presence of war and genocide beyond our borders, and hate based upon our differences within our own communities, how are we to feel emotions such as peace and healing? Clearly, we must find a way to break the cycle of hurt-suffering-anger-hate if we're to transcend the conditions that we find ourselves in.

In the languages of their time, ancient traditions left us precise instructions for how to do just that! Through their words, we're reminded that "life" is nothing more, and nothing less, than a mirror of what we've become within. The key to experiencing our lives as beauty, or as pain, rests solely within our ability to *become* these qualities in each moment of every day. A growing body of scientific evidence gives renewed credibility to such wisdom, and the powerful role that each of us plays in contributing to the healing, or the suffering, in our world.

Late in the 20th century, experiments confirmed that we're bathed in a field of energy that connects us all with the events of our world. Given names that range from the Quantum Hologram to the Mind of God, research has shown that through this energy, the beliefs and prayers *within* us are carried into the world *around* us. Both science and ancient tradition suggest the very same thing: We must *embody* in our lives the very conditions that we wish to *experience* in our world. We find the instructions for a lost mode of prayer that helps us do just that, hidden within some of the most isolated and remote locations remaining on Earth today.

In the spring of 1998, I had the honor of facilitating a 22-day pilgrimage into the monasteries of central Tibet, searching for evidence of an ancient and forgotten form of prayer—the language that speaks to the field that unites all things. The monks and the nuns who live there shared the instructions for a way to pray that was largely lost to the West in the fourth-century biblical edits of the early

Christian Church.[3] Preserved for centuries in the texts and traditions of those living upon the roof of the world, this "lost" mode of prayer has no words or outward expressions. It is based solely in feeling.

Specifically, it invites us to feel as if our prayer has already been answered, rather than feeling powerless and needing to ask for help from a higher source. In recent years, studies have shown that it is this very quality of feeling that does, in fact, "speak" to the field that connects us with the world. Through prayers of feeling, we're empowered to take part in the healing of our lives and relationships, as well as our bodies and our world.

To Do As Angels Do . . .

The key to using this mode of prayer is to recognize the hidden power of beauty, blessing, wisdom, and pain. Each plays a necessary role as part of a greater cycle that allows us to feel, learn, release, and transcend life's deepest hurts. In the words of an unnamed scribe recording the teachings of Jesus nearly 2,000 years ago, we're reminded that the power to change our world, as well as any obstacles that stand between us and that power, live within us. He simply stated, "The most difficult thing of all [to do as humans] is to think the thoughts of angels . . . and to do as angels do."[4]

Prayer is the language of God and the angels. It's also the language we were given to heal life's suffering with wisdom, beauty, and grace. Whether we learn of prayer's power from the Internet today, or from a first-century parchment scroll, the message is the same. Accepting our ability to use such a universal language may well be the greatest challenge of our lives. At the same time, it is the source of our greatest strength. When we know beyond any doubt that we *already* speak the feeling language of prayer, we awaken that part of us that can never be stolen, lost, or taken away. This is the secret of the lost mode of prayer.

— Gregg Braden
Taos, New Mexico

Chapter One

THE FIRST SECRET:
OUR LOST MODE OF PRAYER

*The force that created the unimaginable splendors
and the unimaginable horrors has taken refuge in
us, and it will follow our commands.*

— St. Catherine of Siena

THERE IS SOMETHING "OUT THERE." JUST BEYOND
OUR PERCEPTIONS OF THE EVERYDAY WORLD THERE'S
A PRESENCE, OR FORCE, THAT'S AT ONCE BOTH MYS-
TERIOUS AND COMFORTING. WE TALK ABOUT IT.
WE FEEL IT. WE BELIEVE IN IT AND PRAY TO IT,
PERHAPS WITHOUT EVEN UNDERSTANDING PRE-
CISELY WHAT *IT* IS!

1

Calling it by names that vary from the Web of Creation to the Spirit of God, ancient traditions knew that this presence exists. They also knew how to apply it in their lives. In the words of their time, they left detailed instructions to the people of their future describing how we may use this invisible force to heal our bodies and relationships, and bring peace to our world. Today we know that the language connects all three as a "lost" mode of prayer.

Unlike the traditional prayers that we may have used in the past, however, this technique of prayer has no words. It is based in the silent language of human emotion. It invites us to feel gratitude and appreciation, *as if our prayers have already been answered.* Through this quality of feeling, the ancients believed that we're given direct access to the power of creation: the Spirit of God.

In the 20th century, modern science may have rediscovered the Spirit of God as a field of energy that's different from any other form of energy. It appears to be everywhere, always, and to have existed since the beginning of time. The man widely regarded as the father of quantum physics, Max Planck, stated that the existence of the Field suggests that a great intelligence is responsible for our physical world. "We must assume behind this force the existence of a conscious and intelligent mind." He concluded, simply saying, "This mind is the matrix of all matter."[1] Referring to it by other terms such as the Unity Field, contemporary studies have shown that Planck's matrix does, in fact, have intelligence. Just as the ancients suggested, the Field responds to human emotion!

Regardless of what we call it or how science and religion define it, it's clear that there's something out there—a force, a field, a presence—that is the "great magnet" constantly pulling us toward one another and connecting us to a higher power. Knowing that this force exists, it makes tremendous sense that we'd be able to communicate with it in a way that is meaningful and useful in our lives. Ultimately, we may discover that the same power that heals our deepest hurts and creates peace between nations holds the key to our survival as a species.

The worldwide census that was conducted in 2000 is believed to be the most accurate accounting of our world in recorded history.

3

Among the compelling statistics that the survey revealed about our global family, and perhaps the most telling, is our nearly universal sense that we're here on purpose, and we're not alone. Over 95 percent of the world's population believes in the existence of a higher power. Of that number, over half call that power "God."

The question now is less about whether or not something is "out there," and more about what that "something" means in our lives. How can we speak to the higher power that so many of us believe in? The same traditions that described nature's secrets thousands of years ago answered this question as well. As you'd expect, the language that connects us with God is found in a very common experience that we all share. It is the experience of our feelings and emotions.

When we focus on a certain quality of feeling in our hearts, we're actually using the mode of prayer that was largely forgotten after the now well-publicized biblical edits of the fourth century. The key to using feeling as our prayer-language is simply to understand how prayer works. In the most remote and isolated sanctuaries remaining on Earth today, those

5

least disturbed by modern civilization, we find some of the best-preserved examples of how we may speak to the presence that 95 percent of us believe exists.

Feeling Is the Prayer

I was reeling from what I'd just heard. The cold from the stone floor beneath my knees had found its way through the dampness of the two layers of clothing that I'd worn that morning. Each day on the Tibetan plateau is both summer and winter: summer in the direct high-altitude sun; and winter as the sun disappears behind the jagged peaks of the Himalayas . . . or behind the high temple walls like those that surrounded me. It felt as if there was nothing between my skin and the ancient stones on the floor beneath me, yet I couldn't leave. This was the reason why I'd invited 20 others to join me in a journey that led us halfway around the world. On this day, we found ourselves in some of the most remote, isolated, magnificent, and sacred places of knowledge remaining on Earth today: the monasteries of the Tibetan plateau.

For 14 days we'd acclimated our bodies to altitudes of more than 16,000 feet above sea level. We'd crossed an icy river in hand-hewn wooden barges, and driven for hours peering at one another over our surgical masks, which acted as filters for the dust that floated through the floorboards of our vintage Chinese bus. Although the bus seemed as old as the temples themselves, our translator assured me that it wasn't! Holding on to the seats around us, and even on to one another, we had braced ourselves over washed-away bridges and roadless desert, as we were jarred from the inside out, just to be in this very place in this precise moment. I thought, *Today is not about being warm. Today is a day of answers.*

I focused my attention directly into the eyes of the beautiful and timeless-looking man seated lotus-style in front of me: the abbot of the monastery. Through our translator, I'd just asked him the same question that I'd asked each monk and nun that we'd met throughout our pilgrimage: "When we see your prayers," I began, "what are you *doing?* When we see you tone and chant for 14 and 16 hours a day, when we see the bells, the bowls, the gongs, the chimes, the mudras, and the mantras on the outside, *what is happening to you on the inside?"*

As the translator shared the abbot's reply, a powerful sensation rippled through my body, and I knew that this was the reason we'd come to this place. "You have never seen our prayers," he answered, "because a prayer cannot be seen." Adjusting the heavy wool robes beneath his feet, the abbot continued. "What you have seen is what we do to create the feeling in our bodies. *Feeling is the prayer!"*

The clarity of the abbot's answer sent me reeling. His words echoed the ideas that had been recorded in ancient Gnostic and Christian traditions more than 2,000 years ago. In early translations of the biblical book of John (chapter 16, verse 24, for example), we're invited to empower our prayers by *being* surrounded by [feeling] our desires fulfilled, just as the abbot suggested: "Ask without hidden motive and *be surrounded by your answer.*" For our prayers to be answered, we must transcend the doubt that often accompanies the positive nature of our desire. Following a brief teaching on the power of overcoming such polarities, the words of Jesus recorded in the Nag Hammadi

8

THE

NEW TESTAMENT

OF OUR

LORD AND SAVIOUR JESUS CHRIST

TRANSLATED OUT OF

THE O

T H E

THE FORMER

A M

[Pearl 32

Library remind us that when we do this, and say to the mountain, "'Mountain move away,' it will move away."[2]

If the wisdom was that consistent over such vast periods of time, then it must be useful to us, even today! Using nearly identical language, both the abbot and the scrolls were describing a form of prayer that has been largely forgotten in the West.

Sacred Lessons from the Past

Prayer is perhaps one of the most ancient and mysterious of human experiences. It's also one of the most personal. Even before the word *prayer* appeared in spiritual practices, the oldest records of the Christian and Gnostic traditions used words such as *communion* to describe our ability to speak with the unseen forces of the universe. Prayer is unique to everyone who experiences it. Some estimate that there are as many different ways to pray as there are people who do the praying!

Today, modern prayer researchers have identified four broad categories that are believed to encompass all the many ways that we pray. In no particular order, they are: (1) colloquial, or informal, prayers; (2) petitionary prayers; (3) ritualistic prayers; and (4) meditative prayers.[3] When we pray, the researchers suggest that we use one of these four modes—or a combination.

As good as these descriptions are, and as well as each of these prayers appears to work, there's always been another mode of prayer that this list doesn't account for. This fifth mode of prayer, the "lost mode," is a prayer that's based solely in *feeling*. Rather than the sense of helplessness that often leads us to ask for assistance from a higher power, feeling-based prayer acknowledges our ability to communicate with the intelligent force that 95 percent of us believe in, and participate in the outcome.

Without any words, without our hands held in a certain position or any outward physical expression, this mode of prayer simply invites us to *feel* a clear and powerful feeling as if our prayers have already been answered. Through this intangible "language," we participate in the healing of our bodies, the abundance that comes to our friends and families, and the peace between nations.

Sometimes we see references to this mode of prayer, perhaps without recognizing what

11

we're being shown. In the American Southwest, for instance, ancient stone structures were created in the desert by their builders as "chapels": sacred places where wisdom could be shared and prayers offered. These perfectly circular stone buildings, some submerged and covered deep within the earth, were known as *kivas* (pronounced *KEE-vuhs*). Etched, carved, and painted into the walls of some kivas are clues as to how the lost mode of prayer was used in native traditions.

Inside restored kivas in the Four-Corners area, there are the remnants of the mud plaster that covered the stone structures long ago. Lightly etched into the earthen stucco, we can still see the faint images of rain clouds and lightning hovering over abundant fields of corn. In other places, the walls show outlines that hint at wildlife such as elk and deer, which were abundant in the valleys. In this way, the ancient artists recorded the secret of the lost mode of prayer.

In the places where the prayers were offered, those praying surrounded themselves with the images of the very things that they chose to experience in their lives! Not unlike the scenes of miracles and resurrection that we see in a church or temple today, the images inspired those who were praying with the *feeling* that their prayers had been answered. For them, prayer was a full-body experience, involving all of their senses.

Praying "Rain"

Any uncertainty that I may have had regarding how this principle works disappeared one day in the early 1990s. It had been a time of extreme drought in the high deserts of northern New Mexico, when my native friend David (not his real name) invited me to an ancient stone circle to "pray rain." After meeting at a prearranged location, I followed him on an early-morning hike through a valley that contained more than 100,000 acres of high-desert sage. After walking for a couple of hours, our journey led us to a place that David had been to many times before and knew very well. It was an earthen circle made of stones arranged in perfect geometries of lines and arrows, just the way the hands of its maker had placed them long ago.

"What is this place?" I asked.

"This is the reason that we have come." David laughed. "This stone circle is a medicine wheel that has been here for as long as my people can remember." He continued, "The wheel itself has no power. It serves as a place of focus for the one invoking the prayer. You could think of it as a road map—a map between humans and the forces of this world." Anticipating my next questions, David described how he'd been taught the language of this map from the time that he was a young boy. "Today," he said, "I will travel an ancient path that leads to other worlds. From those worlds, I will do what we came here to do. Today, we pray rain."

I wasn't prepared for what I saw next. I watched carefully as David removed his shoes, gently placed his naked feet into the circle, and honored the four directions and all of his ancestors. Slowly, he placed his hands in front of his face in a praying position, closed his eyes, and became motionless. Oblivious to the heat of the midday desert sun, his breathing slowed and became barely noticeable. After only a few moments, he took a deep breath, opened his eyes to look at me, and said, "Let's go. Our work is finished here."

Expecting to see dancing, or at least some chanting, I was surprised by how quickly his prayer began and then ended. "Already?" I asked. "I thought you were going to pray *for* rain!"

David's reply to my question has been the key that has helped so many to understand this kind of prayer. As he sat on the ground to lace up his shoes, David looked up at me and smiled. "No," he replied. "I said that I would *pray* rain. If I had prayed *for* rain, it could never happen." Later in the day, David explained what he meant by this statement.

He began by describing how the elders of his village had shared the secrets of prayer with him when he was a young boy. The key, he said, is that when we ask for something *to* happen, we give power to what we do not have. Prayers *for* healing empower the sickness. Prayers *for* rain empower the drought. "Continuing to ask *for* these things only gives more power to the things that we would like to change," he said.

I think about David's words often, and what they could mean in our lives today. If we pray *for* world peace, for example, while feeling tremendous anger toward those who lead us into war, or even war itself, we may inadvertently be fueling the very conditions that lead to the opposite of peace! With half of the world's nations now engaged in armed conflict, I often wonder what role millions of well-intentioned prayers *for* peace each day may be playing, and how a slight shift in perspective could possibly change that role.

Looking back at David, I asked, "If you didn't pray *for* rain, then what did you do?"

"It's simple," he replied. "I began to have the *feeling* of what rain feels like. I felt the feeling of rain on my body, and what it feels like to stand with my naked feet in the mud of our village plaza because there has been so much rain. I smelled the smells of rain on the earthen walls in our village, and felt what it feels like to walk through fields of corn chest high because there has been so much rain."

David's explanation made perfect sense. He was engaging all of his senses—the hidden powers of thought, feeling, and emotion that set us apart from all other forms of life—in addition to the senses of smell, sight, taste, and touch that connect us to the world. In doing so, he was using the powerful and ancient language that "speaks" to nature. It was the next part of his explanation that touched my

17

scientific mind, as well as my heart, and truly resonated with me.

Following the prayers of rain, he described how feelings of thanks and appreciation were the completion of the prayers, like the "amen" of Christianity. Rather than giving thanks for what he created, however, David told me that he felt grateful for the opportunity to participate in creation. "Through our thanks, we honor all possibilities, while bringing the ones we choose to this world."

Research has shown that it's precisely this quality of gratitude and appreciation that re-leases the life-affirming chemistry of powerful hormones in our bodies and strengthens our immune systems. It's these chemical changes *within* us that quantum effects carry *beyond* our bodies through the conduit of the mysterious substance that appears to connect all of creation. In the simplicity of a knowledge offered long ago, David had just shared this sophisticated inner technology, as the wisdom of our lost mode of prayer.

If you have not already done so, I now invite you to try this mode of prayer for yourself. Think of something that you'd like to experience in your life—anything. It may be the healing of a physical condition for you or someone else, abundance for your family, or finding the perfect person to share your life with. Whatever you're thinking of, rather than asking for it to become present in your life, feel as though it has already happened. Breathe deeply, and feel the fullness of your prayer fulfilled in every detail, in every way.

Now, feel the gratitude for what your life is like with this prayer already answered. Note the ease and release that comes from the giving of thanks, rather than the longing and yearning that comes from asking for help! The subtle difference between the ease and the longing is the power that sets *asking* apart from *receiving*.

Dreaming in the Mind of God

A growing number of discoveries now confirms a previously unrecognized form of energy that may explain why prayers like David's work. This subtle energy field works

19

differently from the kinds of energy we're typically used to measuring. While it's not entirely electrical or magnetic, these familiar forces are a part of the unified field that appears to bathe all of creation. Because awareness of this field is so new, scientists have yet to agree on a single name for it. It's identified in research papers and books by names ranging from the Quantum Hologram and Nature's Mind, to the Mind of God, and often simply the "Field." Whatever we choose to call it, this energy appears to be the living canvas upon which the events of our lives are inscribed!

20

To help visualize what such a field may look like, scientists sometimes describe it as a tightly woven web that makes up the underlying fabric of creation—literally, the blanket of the Mind of God. Of the many ways that it may be defined, I find it most helpful to think of the Field as the "stuff" that lives in the nothing. Whenever we look into the space between us and another person—or between anything else for that matter—and believe that the space is empty, the Field is there. Whether we're thinking about the space between the nucleus and the first orbit of an electron in the old models of an atom, or the vast distances between stars and galaxies that appear empty to us, the size of the space makes no difference. In the nothing, the Field is there.

The modern recognition that the Field exists now gives us a language, and a context, to make sense of spiritual wisdom in scientific conversations. The Field, for example, is believed to be the place that the ancients referred to as "heaven." It is the place where souls go when we die, where we dream when we sleep, and the home of consciousness.

The existence of a field of energy that connects all of creation changes the way in which science has thought about our world for more than 100 years. From the results of the famous Michelson and Morley experiment[4] performed in 1887, scientists concluded that the things that happen in our world are unrelated—what someone does in one part of the world has no effect upon someone else in another part of the world. Now we know that this is simply not true! Through the blanket of energy that bathes our world, we're all linked in ways that we're only beginning to understand.

21

The Mirror That Doesn't Lie

In addition to connecting all things, ancient traditions suggest that the Field provides us with a reflection, an *outer mirror* of our *inner experiences*. As a pulsating, shimmering, living substance, the Field serves as a feedback mechanism of sorts. Through it, creation reflects our innermost feelings and thoughts in the form of our relationships, careers, and health. In the mirror, we can see our true beliefs—*not just what we like to think we believe!*

To help visualize how this mirror works, I'm sometimes reminded of the "living" water in the science-fiction movie *The Abyss*. Set in the dark and uncharted depths of the ocean floor, a mysterious life-form makes itself known to the marooned crew of a deep-sea exploration vessel. (I'll be brief and general here because I don't want to spoil the story if you haven't already seen it.) The nonphysical energy of the alien-like presence must express itself through something physical, and so uses the most abundant medium available at the bottom of the ocean: seawater. As an intelligent and seemingly endless tube of seawater, it finds its way into the disabled vessel, and then snakes its way through the corridors and doorways until it finds the crew huddled together in one room to conserve power.

This is where the mirror comes in. As the watery life-form rises up from the floor and one end of the tube looks directly into the faces of the crew at eye level, a remarkable thing begins to happen. Every time one of the crew looks at the end of the tube, it mirrors that person's face exactly as it appears in the moment. As the human face smiles, the water-tube smiles. When the human face laughs, that laugh is mirrored in the water. The tube has no judgment of what it's being shown, and it doesn't try to enhance or change what's there in any way. It just reflects to the person in front of it what that person is in the moment.

The Field of God's Mind appears to work in precisely this way, and it includes the reflection of what we are inside, as well as the way we portray ourselves on the outside.

"Feeling is the prayer," the Tibetan abbot had said, paralleling the teachings of the great masters from the Native American, as well as the Christian and Jewish, traditions. I thought, *How powerful! How beautiful! How simple!* Feeling is the language that the Mind

23

of God recognizes. Feeling is the language that David used to invite rain to the desert. Because it happens in a way that's so straightforward and so literal, it's easy to see why we may have believed that this principle would be more complicated than it really is. It's just as easy to see how we could have missed it altogether.

Consciousness Creates!

The Field simply mirrors the quality of our feelings as the experiences of our lives. In the words of another time, 2,500-year-old texts describe this wisdom precisely, and also indicate how it's even older than the pages it's recorded on. *The Essene Gospel of Peace,* for example, says: "My children, know you not that the Earth, and all that dwells therein, is but a *reflection* of the kingdom of the heavenly Father? [Author's emphasis]"[5] Just as ripples radiate from the place where a stone is thrown into a pool of water, our sometimes-unconscious thoughts, feelings, emotions, and beliefs create the "disturbances" in the Field that become the blueprints for our lives.

25

It's easy to discount the power of this principle because of how few words it takes to explain it. Without the heaviness of technical jargon or scientific double-talk, the ancients related a simple understanding of how the events of everyday life are directly linked to the quality of our feelings. Through the clarity of this profound wisdom, the responsibility for our health, and for peace, is taken beyond the realm of "chance" events and "bad luck" and placed within our grasp.

While the idea of an ever-present field of intelligence is nothing new, modern physicists have now elevated the concept to a higher level of consideration and mainstream acceptance. Perhaps renowned Princeton University physicist John Wheeler, Ph.D., who was a contemporary of Albert Einstein, has best described the revolutionary physics of an energy that connects all of creation. I remember reading an interview with Wheeler in 2002 following his recovery from a serious illness. When he was asked what direction his work would now take, he responded that he viewed his illness and recovery as an opportunity. It was the catalyst inviting him to focus upon the single question that had eluded him for so long.

"What is that question?" the interviewer asked. Wheeler replied that he planned to dedicate his life to understanding the relationship between consciousness and the universe. In the world of traditional physics, this statement, in and of itself, is enough to shake the foundations of accepted theory and cause the fathers of modern textbooks to roll over in their graves! Historically, concepts about consciousness and the fabric of the universe aren't used in the same sentence.

Wheeler, however, didn't stop there. In subsequent years, he has elaborated upon his theories, suggesting that consciousness is more than a by-product of the universe. He proposes that we live in a "participatory" universe. "We are part of a universe that is a work in progress," he says. "We are tiny patches of the universe looking at itself, *and building itself.*" The implications of Wheeler's statements are vast. In the language of 20th-century science, he's reiterating what ancient traditions stated millennia ago: It is consciousness that creates!

When we peer into the void of the universe in search of its limits, or into the quantum world of the atom, the very act of us looking puts something there for us to see. The

27

anticipation of consciousness expecting to see something—the *feeling* that something is there to see—is the act that creates.

Going further than the statement of John Wheeler, one of the most respected scientists of the 20th, and now the 21st, century, the ancient texts elaborate upon the idea that we create by observing with one important—and often overlooked—detail. They suggest that it's the quality of our beliefs *while we're looking* that determines what our consciousness creates. In other words, if we view our bodies and the world through a lens of separateness, anger, hurt, and hate, then the quantum mirror reflects these qualities back to us as anger in our families, illness in our bodies, and war between nations. If feeling is the prayer, as David and the abbot both suggested, then when we pray *for* something to happen, while feeling as if that same something is missing in our lives, we may actually be denying ourselves the very blessings we hoped to create.

On the other hand, if we can view ourselves from a perspective of unity, appreciation, wisdom, and love, then these are the qualities that we may expect to see mirrored as loving, supportive families and communities, and peace and cooperation between nations. Imagine the possibilities. . . .

Using What We Know

This principle of a neutral and participatory universe may begin to answer the question asked by so many: "If prayer is so powerful, then why does it seem like the more we pray for peace, for example, the worse things seem to become?" Without bias or judgment, is it possible that what we see as an unsettled world of chaos is simply the Field mirroring our belief that peace is missing—our "Please, *let* there be peace" echoed back to us as chaos? If so, then the really good news is that our newfound understanding of how the mirror works encourages us to change what we say to the Field.

This is why the lost mode of prayer can make such a powerful contribution to our lives. Whether we're talking about a lasting relationship, the perfect job, or the healing of disease, the principle is the same. We're simply reminded that the "stuff" that underlies all of creation is a malleable essence that reflects

29

what we feel. So what we choose to create, we must first feel as a reality. If we can feel it in our hearts—not just think it, but also *really feel it*—then it's possible in our lives!

In the example of peace, for instance, we know that it always exists and is present somewhere. The same is true for health and happiness; they always exist somewhere, or have existed, in some form in our lives. The key is to hone in on these positive qualities of our experience, viewing the world as it already is, with appreciation and gratitude. By doing so, we open the door to a greater possibility. We have already seen what happens when millions of people pray *for* peace to come to our world. What would happen if millions of people felt the feelings of gratitude and appreciation for the peace that's already here? It's certainly worth a try!

While for some people this is a very unconventional way to think about their relationship to the world, for others it is perfectly aligned with their beliefs and past experiences. Scientific studies support these principles and have found that when tension is relieved within a group of people through meditation and prayer, the effects are felt *be-yond* the immediate group.

In 1972, 24 cities in the United States with populations over 10,000 experienced meaningful changes in their communities when as few as one percent (100 people) participated. These and similar studies led to a landmark study, the International Peace Project in the Middle East, which was published in *The Journal of Conflict Resolution* in 1988.[6] During the Israeli-Lebanese war of the early 1980s, researchers trained a group of people to "feel" peace in their bodies rather than simply think about peace in their minds or pray for peace to occur.

On specific days of the month, at specific times each day, these people were positioned throughout the war-torn areas of the Middle East. During the window of time that they were feeling peace, terrorist activities stopped, crimes against people lessened, emergency-room visits declined, and traffic accidents dropped off in number. When the people stopped expressing these feelings, the statistics reversed. These studies confirmed the earlier results: When a small percentage of the population achieved peace within themselves, that peace was reflected in the world around them.

The findings took into account the days of the week, holidays, and even lunar cycles, and the data was so consistent that the researchers were able to identify how many people are needed to share the experience of peace before it is mirrored in their world. The number is the square root of one percent of the population. This formula produces numbers that are smaller than we might expect. For example, in a city of one million people, the number is about 100. In a world of 6 billion people, the number is only about 8,000! This number represents only the minimum needed to begin the process. The more people there are, the faster an effect is created.

While these and similar studies obviously deserve more exploration, they show that there's an effect here that's beyond chance. The quality of our innermost beliefs clearly influences the quality of our outer world. From this perspective, everything from the healing of our bodies to the peace between nations, from our success in business, relationships, and careers to the failure of marriages and the breakup of families, must be considered as reflections of us, and of the meaning that we give to the experiences of our lives.

In addition to answering our earlier question about "what is happening in the world," the existence of the Unity Field invites us to go one step further. Coupled with the knowledge of feeling-based prayer, this modern/ancient wisdom shows us what we can do to make things better. If the world and our bodies are reflecting our thoughts, feelings, emotions, and beliefs, then with record numbers of broken homes, failed relationships, job losses, and threats of war at present, how we feel about our world takes on an importance greater than ever before.

It's clear that for the mirror of our world to reflect positive, life-affirming, and lasting change, we must give the mirror something to work with. This is the subtle yet powerful relationship between the language of prayer and the Mind of God that unites all of creation. Rather than attempting to make the world bend to our wishes, feeling-based prayer changes *us*. We bend, and the world spontaneously reflects our improvements.

Perhaps this insight is best summed up in the single statement of the 19th-century Danish philosopher Søren Kierkegaard: "Prayer does not change God, but it changes him who prays." So how do we change the way we feel about life's hurts? This is where the work really begins!

The World As a Mirror

Without bias or judgment, it is the spiritual mirror of the Mind of God that reflects back to us what we've become in our thoughts, feelings, emotions, and beliefs. In other words, our inner experiences of hurt and fear, as well as those of love and compassion, become the theme for the kind of relationships that we find in our jobs and friendships, as well as our expressions of abundance, and even our health. The key in this way of looking at the world is that what we "do" as the outward expression of life is less of a factor than what we "become"—the way we *feel* about what we do.

For clarity, let's look at an example. Let's say that you or an acquaintance is attending a spiritual workshop describing the inner principles of feeling, emotion, and prayer, and the role that these inner experiences of peace play in our world. Due to unforeseen circumstances, the workshop has run overtime by 30 minutes or so. If you bolt out of the room toward the parking lot before the lights come

up and the doors even open, carelessly back out of your parking space doing a three-point turn in which you bump into three other cars, and then race down the freeway endangering your life and the lives of others as you swerve across all three lanes to make the exit because you're late for a peace rally, then you've missed the point!

Perhaps the knowledge of this subtle yet powerful mirror can help us make sense of what we seem to be experiencing in the world today. From this way of looking at things, what we see portrayed in movies, news media, and the world around us is a reflection of the beliefs that we've nourished in our families, homes, and communities *in the past.*

37

Similarly, the powerful examples of love, compassion, and dedication that we see in the presence of war or natural disaster are also something more than the acts of a few people who carry out humanitarian efforts in these areas. They reflect the best of what's possible when we find a way to see beyond the hurt that life has shown us. The power of recognizing the world as a reflection of our beliefs is that if such a relationship truly exists, it must work for healing beliefs as well as destructive ones. In this way, we're all part of the change that we'd like to see in our world. The key is in recognizing the language of the change!

Chapter Two

THE SECOND SECRET:
HURT IS THE TEACHER, WISDOM IS THE LESSON

If you bring forth that which you have within you, it will save you. If you do not, it will destroy you.

— The Gospel of Thomas

AT FIRST, THE IMAGES ON THE TELEVISION SCREEN MADE LITTLE SENSE TO ME. ALTHOUGH THE LANDSCAPE WAS UNFAMILIAR, WITHIN THE PAST WEEKS GRAPHIC SCENES LIKE THE ONE IN THIS BROADCAST HAD BECOME ALL TOO COMMON: THERE WAS CHAOS, as people of all ages ran in every direction, dirty, burned, and terrified. I'd just come back to my hotel room following a full day of teaching in Sydney, Australia, when I turned on the news to catch up on the day. As I moved closer to the screen, I began to understand what I was seeing.

The local stations were carrying a live video feed from School Number 1 in Beslan, Russia, raw and unedited. Only a few days earlier, hundreds of children and adults had been taken hostage by terrorists on the first day of the new school year. While the standoff had dragged on for days, obviously something had changed. When the dust settled, the final numbers of the tragedy were staggering. Of the approximately 1,200 hostages that had been held captive in the school's gymnasium, nearly 350 had been killed. Over half of those were children, dead for no apparent reason other than the senseless rationale of a handful of angry people.

The human details that emerged from individual families gave perspective to the day. In almost every street of the city, people had either lost someone personally or knew the relatives of someone who was killed. Many were burying more than one family member. One resident, Vitally Kaloev, buried his entire family: his wife, son, and daughter. Pastor Teymuraz Totiev and his wife buried four of their five children: Boris, 8; Albina, 11; Luba, 12; and Larissa, 14. Their fifth daughter, Madina, had been injured and was recovering at their home. In a tragic twist of fate, Pastor Totiev's brother, also a pastor, and his wife lost two of their three children.

Similar to the overwhelming shock of lives lost on September 11 in New York City, the magnitude of what happened at Beslan was almost too much for those looking on to grasp. Even people whose faith had traditionally been a touchstone for others in times of hardship found their beliefs tested by the ruthlessness of the tragedy.

Rowan Williams, the archbishop of Canterbury, admitted that the sight of innocent children being massacred led him momentarily to doubt his faith in God. "So where was God at Beslan?"[1] he asked. With these words, Archbishop Williams publicly expressed the hurt that many felt privately. The shock, disbelief, and pain of Beslan's residents was carried via the media and experienced by others

41

throughout the world. On that day, millions of people's hearts, minds, and prayers were with the Russian people as they shared the universal experience of hurt.

Whether it's on a global scale, such as Russia's Beslan or America's September 11, or in our personal lives, how we deal with loss and tragedy is a question that each of us will have to answer during our lifetime. Although the experience of hurt is universal, what we do with our hurt is not.

If we allow the pain of life's disappointments and losses to linger unresolved, it can destroy our health, our lives, and the very relationships that we most cherish. If, on the other hand, we can find wisdom in our hurt, we can give new meaning to the most painful experiences. In doing so, we become better as people— for ourselves, for our families, and for our communities. This is the way we build a better world.

How Much Can We Bear?

The knowledge of the power that awaits us beyond our suffering has been recognized and honored for centuries. It was described nearly 2,000 years ago in the second-century Nag Hammadi Library through words that are as meaningful today as they were at the time of their writing. Among the ancient Gnostic texts are passages suggesting that our vulnerability to suffering is the doorway to healing and life. In the Gospel of Thomas, one of the most inspiring of the recovered texts, the author describes the power of our vulnerability as part of a discourse from Jesus: "Blessed is the man who has suffered and found life."

In another portion of the teaching, Jesus states: "That which you have will save you if you bring it forth from yourselves."[2] Ultimately, the love that lives within each of us is the source of all healing that we experience. To feel our love, however, we must be vulnerable to our pain. Hurt is one way for us to know how deeply we can feel. Our capacity to feel pain within ourselves, as well as have empathy for the pain of others, shows us how deeply we can love. Simply put, hurt is the price that we sometimes pay to discover that we already have the love we need to heal ourselves. Sometimes, merely knowing of the relationship between wisdom,

43

hurt, and love is enough to catapult us to the other end of the extreme and to healing.

As the stories of Beslan unfolded over the course of hours and days, a single question emerged from the Russian people. Following the terrorist takeover of their interior ministry building that had killed 92 people, the almost simultaneous explosions of two commercial airliners only moments after takeoff killing all 90 on board, and now the death toll of more than 350 in Beslan, people of that country were asking, "How much pain can we bear?" According to ancient traditions, the answer to these questions is brief, clear, and straightforward. The great challenges of life appear to us when, *and only when,* we have everything we need to survive and heal from the experience.

Mothers throughout the world have passed down this time-tested insight from generation to generation in a single phrase of comfort and clarity: "God never gives us more than we can bear." In this uncomplicated assertion, we're being offered a promise that has withstood the test of time and can now be verified by science. *We already have all we need to survive life's tests.* While we may find comfort and insight in self-help books, magazine articles, and seminars, the spiritual tools we need already exist within us.

The answer to "How much pain can we bear?" may appear deceptively simple. The reason *why* this holds true requires a little more explanation. As is so often the case with patterns, nature provides a model for the way our emotions and experiences work in our lives.

Balance: It's Not All That It's Cracked Up to Be

In the early part of the 20th century, naturalist R. N. Elliott suggested that nature follows patterns that may be recognized, charted, and predicted with numbers. From the rise and fall of populations to the cycles of weather, his theories implied that nature tends toward balance. Viewing humankind as part of nature, Elliott reasoned that our lives, including the way we spend money in the stock market, should follow natural patterns as well—patterns that may be modeled and charted visually. Elliott applied his theories successfully to cycles of business and finance, and his work became the basis for one of the most successful stock-market prediction tools in history, later known as the Elliott Wave Theory.

It should come as no surprise then, that our spending habits—or any other patterns in our lives for that matter—can be represented mathematically. Numbers are believed to be the universal language that describes everything from the origin of galaxies to the swirls of milk in a cup of coffee. Following this reasoning, it also makes sense that the same processes describing the visible world of nature may also be viewed as *metaphors* for the invisible world of feelings and emotions as well! This is precisely the case with fractal mathematics.

As a relatively recent innovation in the way we describe our world, fractal geometry mixes mathematics with art to show us visually what the equations have only implied in the past. From rugged mountain peaks to blood vessels, from coastlines to particles of lint, fractals allow us to model many of the things that we see in nature. In doing so, we're transported beyond the sometimes dry and sterile world of numbers on paper, to the beauty and mystery of seeing those numbers as a language that illustrates our world.

One of the most commonly recognized forms of the fractal patterns is known as the Mandelbrot equation, or the Mandelbrot set. Discovered by the mathematician Benoit Mandelbrot in the late 1970s, once this "living" equation is set into motion on our computer screen, it grows and evolves over short periods of time as a beautiful and ever-changing series of curves, swirls, and lacy patterns. In doing so, it illustrates the never-ending dance between balance and chaos in nature. When we watch the colors and patterns change in the simulated images, we're actually seeing a powerful representation of the way our emotional relationships play out in life as well.

The patterns that appear and then disappear represent the relationships and careers, and all of the joy and sadness that come and go throughout our lives. Just as the computer images show us that balance can come only when all of the patterns are in place to support it, we can experience our greatest tests, as well as accept our greatest gifts, only when all of the pieces are in place to do so. As symbols for our never-ending dance of opposites—give-and-take, contraction and expansion, hurt and healing—these powerful images tell the story of how nature is always moving toward or away from perfect balance. In doing so, we see in pictures what we experience in real life.

It is only when we've learned everything that we need, and we have all of the tools to survive and heal in our "spiritual toolbox," that we can draw to us the romances, career changes, business partners, and friendships that allow us to apply what we've learned. Until we have our tools, we'll never have the experience! Another way of saying this is that if life is showing us hurt, disappointment, loss, and betrayal, we must already have what we need to get through our experience.

The key is that rather than balance being the goal, what we think of as "balance" is actually the trigger that invites the change! We see this in the fractals, as well as in our lives. It is *only* when the patterns on our computer screen find perfect balance—when the patterns are equal—that they begin to come apart, only to evolve into newer patterns of even greater balance. Our lives appear to work in precisely the same way.

Unlike the brief life span of the fractals, however, there appears to be no time limit on how long it takes us to accumulate spiritual

49

tools in our lives. While digital pictures break down and reassemble again in a matter of minutes, it may take months, years, decades, or even an entire lifetime for a particular cycle to complete within us. Along the way we may find ourselves repeating patterns, experiencing the same kind of jobs, the same kind of friendships, or the same kind of romances until the "Aha!" experience ignites within us the realization of why we "do" the things that we "do."

Have you ever wondered, for example, why you can start a new job in a new city with new co-workers and, except for the changing names, find yourself in precisely the same situations that caused you to leave the last job in the last city? Patterns aren't necessarily "good" or "bad"—there's no judgment implied here. If you find yourself playing out a familiar old pattern in a new setting, this is simply an opportunity to recognize what it might be saying about your life. Recognizing situations like this one gives you the chance to become a better person.

The key idea here is that you can be "tested" in life only when you're ready. Whether or not we're conscious of this principle, no matter what life brings our way, when we find a "crisis" at our doorstep, we already have everything we need to solve the problem, heal the hurt, and survive the experience. We must, because it is nature's way!

From the Highest of the Highs to the Lowest of the Lows

No one is immune to the cycles of balance and change. Regardless of how large our families are, how many friends we have, how many books we've written, or how successful we've become, we all have a trigger point that invites change into our lives. Interestingly, the trigger appears to be different for everyone. While we may believe that we have neatly arranged life as something that we can regulate and control, all the while each experience and every relationship is training and preparing us for something that may be beyond our control.

In doing so, we move ever closer to the moment when we'll be given the opportunity to demonstrate our mastery over our betrayals, violated trusts, and hot-button issues. It's only after we've put our last spiritual tool in place to create the balance, however, that we

51

signal our readiness. It is our balance that says, "Hey! I'm ready. Bring it on!" Now we're ready to demonstrate to the universe what we've learned.

Until we've learned from experience, both consciously and unconsciously, our tests may be so subtle that we don't even recognize them as tests! It's only when we realize what the betrayals and broken promises of our past have shown us that we gain the wisdom and skills that allow us to heal the patterns and move on in life.

The pioneering Buddhist teacher Lama Surya Das *(Awakening the Buddha Within, Letting Go of the Person You Used to Be)* describes how powerful the hurt and sorrowful times in our lives can be. "All life contains both joy and sorrow," he begins. "We would like to concentrate on the joy and forget the sorrow, but how much more spiritually skillful it is to use everything we meet in life as grist for the mill of awakening." Sometimes the "grist" of life comes to us in ways we least expect!

During the high-tech boom of the early 1990s, Gerald (not his real name) was an engineer in Silicon Valley, California. He had two beautiful young daughters and was married to an equally beautiful wife. They'd been together for nearly 15 years. When I met him, his company had recently given him an award for his fifth year with them as a senior troubleshooter for a specialized kind of software. His position had made him a valuable asset to the company, and the need for his expertise extended well beyond the typical 8-to-5 workday.

To meet the demand for his skills, Gerald began to work late evenings and weekends, and to travel to trade shows and expos out of town with his software. Before long, he found himself spending more time with his co-workers than he did with his family. I could see the hurt in his eyes as he described how they'd grown apart. By the time Gerald arrived home in the evenings, his wife and children were sleeping, and he was at his office in the morning before they even began their day. Soon he began to feel like a stranger in his own home. He knew more about the families of people in his office than he did his own.

That's when Gerald's life took a dramatic turn. He happened to come to see me for a counseling session while I was writing a book describing how the "mirrors" of relationships play out in our lives. More than 2,200 years ago, the authors of the Dead Sea Scrolls identified seven specific patterns that we may expect to see in our interactions with other people. As Gerald's story unfolded, it was clear that he was describing one of them, which is life's reflection of our greatest fear, commonly known as the "Dark Night of the Soul."

Among the engineers in Gerald's office was a brilliant young programmer, a woman about his age. He'd found himself teamed up with this woman for assignments that sometimes lasted for days at a time and which took them to cities throughout the country. Before long, he felt like he knew her better than he did his own wife. At this point in the story, I suspected that I knew where it would end. What I did not know was why Gerald was so upset, and what was about to happen to him.

Before long, he believed that he was in love with his co-worker and made the choice to leave his wife and daughters to begin a new life with her. This decision made perfect sense at the time, as they had so much in common. In a few short weeks, however, his new partner was transferred to a project in Los Angeles. By calling in a few favors, Gerald was able to finagle a transfer to the same office.

Immediately, things began to go wrong, and Gerald found that he'd lost more than he'd bargained for. Friends that he and his wife had known for years suddenly became distant and unavailable. His co-workers thought he was "off the wall" for leaving the position and projects that he'd worked so hard for. Even his parents were angry that he'd broken up the family. Although he was hurt, Gerald rationalized that this was simply the price for change. He was off to a great new life. What more could he ask for?

This is where the mirror of balance and the Dark Night of the Soul come in. Just as everything appeared to be falling into place, Gerald discovered that everything was actually falling apart! Within weeks, his new love announced that their relationship wasn't what she'd expected. She ended it suddenly and asked him to leave. Just like that, he was on his own, alone and devastated. "After all that I've done for *her,* how could she?" he moaned.

He'd left his wife, his children, his friends, and his job. In short, he'd left everything that he loved.

Soon he began to perform poorly at his job. Following several warnings and a less-than-stellar performance review, his department eventually laid him off. As Gerald's story unfolded, it was clear what had really happened: His life had gone from the highest of highs, with all of the prospects of a new relationship, new job, and greater income, to the lowest of lows, as all of those dreams disappeared. The night that Gerald came to see me, he was asking a single question: "What happened?" How could things that looked so good turn so bad?

57

Our Dark Night of the Soul: Recognizing the Trigger

By the time I met him, Gerald had lost everything he loved. The reason why is the key to this story. Rather than releasing the things he loved *because* he felt complete and was moving on, he made his choices only when he believed that there was something better to take their place. In other words, he played it safe. Because of his fear that he might not find anything better, he physically stayed with his marriage long after he'd left his family emotionally. There's a subtle yet significant difference between leaving our jobs, friends, and romances because we're complete, and staying with them because of the fear that there's nothing else for us.

There can be a tendency in all kinds of relationships to cling to the status quo until something better comes along. This attachment may come from being unaware of what we're doing, or it may exist because we're afraid to rock the boat and face the uncertainty of not knowing what comes next. Although it may very well represent a pattern of which we're unconscious, it's a pattern, nonetheless. Whether it's a job, a romance, or our lifestyle, we can find ourselves in a holding pattern where we aren't really happy, yet have never honestly communicated this to the people in our lives. So even while the world believes that our lives are business as usual, inside we may be screaming for change and feeling frustrated because we don't know how to share this need with those who are close to us.

This is a pattern that builds negativity. Our true feelings are often disguised as tension, hostility, or sometimes just being absent from the relationship. Each day we go through the motions of our job, or of sharing our life and home with another person, while we're emotionally distant and off in another world. Whether our problem is with a boss, a lover, or even our self, we rationalize, compromise, and wait. Then one day, just like that—*boom!*—*it* happens. Seemingly from out of nowhere, the very things that we've waited for and longed for in our lives suddenly appear. When they do, we may lunge for them like there's no tomorrow.

In Gerald's case, when he moved to a new city with his new relationship, he left behind an unresolved void into which his world collapsed. Now, having lost all that he loved, Gerald was sitting across from me with huge tears rolling down his cheeks. "How can I get my job and my family back? Just tell me what to do!"

As I handed him the box of tissues that I kept on a nearby table for moments just like this one, I said something that caught Gerald completely off guard: "This time in your life isn't about getting back what you've lost," I began, "although that may be just what happens. What

59

you've created for yourself goes much deeper than your job and your family. You've just awakened a force within you that may become your most powerful ally." I continued, "When you've come through this experience, you'll have a new confidence that's unshakable. You've entered a time that the ancients recognized and called the Dark Night of the Soul."

Gerald wiped his eyes and sat back in his chair. "What do you mean, the 'Dark Night of the Soul'?" he asked. "How come I've never heard of it?"

"A Dark Night of the Soul is a time in your life when you'll be drawn into a situation that represents what, for you, are your worst fears," I answered. "A time like this generally comes when you least expect it, and usually without warning. The thing is," I continued, "you can only be drawn into this dynamic when your mastery of life signals that you're ready. Then, just when it looks like life is perfect, the balance that you've achieved is the signal that you're ready for change. The lure to create the change will be something that you long for in life, something that you simply can't resist. Otherwise, you'd never take the leap!"

"Do you mean a lure like a new relationship?" Gerald asked.

"Precisely like a new relationship," I replied. "A relationship is the kind of catalyst that promises we'll move forward in life." Going on, I explained how even if we know that we're perfectly capable of surviving whatever life throws our way, it's not our nature to wake up one morning and say, "Hmm . . . today I think I'll give away all that I love and hold dear in order to enter my Dark Night of the Soul." We just don't seem to work that way. As is so often the case, the great tests of our Dark Night seem to come when we least expect them.

A few years ago, I ran into a friend who'd just left a career, family, friends, and a relationship in his home state to move to the wilderness of northern New Mexico. I asked him why he'd left so much behind to come to the isolation of the high desert. He began by telling me that he'd come to the mountains to find his spiritual path. In the next breath, he described that he hadn't been able to begin his path, however, because nothing was going right. He was having problems with business, family, and the friends that he'd left behind. His frustration was obvious.

I've learned that there are no accidents in life, and that every obstacle we experience is part of a greater pattern. As I listened to his story, the desire of my "man brain" to fix things in life compelled me to offer my perspective. "Maybe this *is* your spiritual path," I suggested. "Maybe the way that you solve each problem is the path that you came here to find."

He looked back as he was walking away, and simply said, "Hmm . . . maybe it is. . . . "

The possibility that life brings us exactly what we need, precisely when we need it, makes perfect sense. Just as we cannot fill a cup with water until we turn the faucet to "on," having a full emotional toolbox is the trigger that signals the faucet of life to bring on change. Until we trigger the flow, nothing can happen. The other side of this dynamic is that when we do find ourselves in a Dark Night of the Soul, it may be reassuring to know that the only way we could have gotten to such a place in life is that *we* are the ones who flipped the switch! Knowingly or not, we're always ready for whatever life may serve up.

Our Greatest Fears

The purpose of the Dark Night of the Soul is for us to experience and heal our own great fears. The really interesting thing about the Dark Night is that, because everyone's fears are different, what looks like a frightening experience for one person may be no big deal to someone else. For example, Gerald admitted that his worst fear was being left alone. I'd spoken with a woman earlier the same evening, however, who told me that "being alone" was her greatest joy.

It's not uncommon for someone who fears being alone to become a master at relationships in which they'll experience their fear. Gerald, for example, described romances, friendships, and jobs in his past that could never have lasted in a million years! When each one ended, he believed that the relationships had "failed." In reality, his relationships were so successful that each one allowed him to see his greatest fear of being alone come to pass. Because he had never healed, or even recognized the patterns in his life before, however, he found himself in situations where his fear became less and less subtle. Ultimately, life led him to the point where his fear was so evident that he had to address it before he could continue.

While we may go through many Dark Nights of the Soul throughout our lifetimes, the first one is usually the toughest. It's also probably the most powerful agent of change. Once we understand *why* we hurt so much, the experience begins to take on new meaning. As we recognize the signposts of a Dark Night, we can say, "Aha! I know that pattern! Yup, it's definitely a Dark Night of the Soul all right. Now, what is it that I'm being asked to master?"

I know people who are so empowered once they heal their Dark Night experiences that they almost dare the universe to bring on the next one. They do so simply because they know that if they've survived the first one, they can survive anything. It's only when we have such experiences without understanding what they are or why we're having them that we can find ourselves locked into years, or even lifetimes, of a pattern that can literally steal the very things from us that we hold most dear, such as life itself.

Is it possible that unresolved hurt could shorten, or even end, a life? The answer may surprise you!

Why Do We Die?

Have you ever wondered why we die? Aside from obvious reasons such as war, murder, accidents, natural disasters, and poor lifestyle choices, what is the real, natural cause of death in humans? If we are, as spiritual traditions suggest, spirits of God in bodies of earth, and if, as medical science believes, our cells are capable of healing and replacing themselves multiple times, then what is our body's "running down" really all about? Why is it that the odds of continuing a healthy, vital, and meaningful life seem to work against us as we pass what is often considered "midlife" and approach the 100-year mark?

I've asked this question many times in workshops throughout the world. Almost immediately, once the reasons listed above are

65

acknowledged, people tell me that "old age" is what takes our lives. "We just get old, and things stop working" is a typical response that I hear. At first glance, research into the medical reasons for death seems to corroborate this.

This perspective may best be summarized by the very first sentence of an article in the *General Health Encyclopedia* titled "Aging Changes in Organs, Tissues, and Cells": "Most people realize that vital organs begin to lose function with aging."[3] I confess that I may not be among that majority! As a matter of fact, the more I research the way our bodies are made and how they work, the more convinced I am that there's something else involved in aging—something that's not being accounted for in our present medical model.

Later in the same article, another statement opens the door to this very possibility. The author acknowledges that the reasons our bodies break down as we get older aren't completely understood. "No theory sufficiently explains all of the changes of the aging process." In other words, we still don't really know precisely why we deteriorate as time passes. While, in all probability, each of us will leave this world at some point, is it possible that we're outgrowing the need to age, suffer, and die for the reasons people traditionally accept?

We Are Miracles Built to Last!

Among scientists, medical professionals, and scholars alike, there's agreement that our bodies have a miraculous ability to sustain life. Of the estimated 50 trillion or so cells that live within the average human, most are documented with the ability to repair and reproduce themselves many times throughout our lifespan. In other words, we're constantly replacing and rebuilding ourselves from the inside out.

67

There appear to be two exceptions to the phenomenon of cell reproduction. Interestingly, these are the cells of the two centers that are most closely identified with the spiritual qualities that make us who we are: our brain cells and our heart cells. Although studies have shown that the cells of these organs *may* have the ability to reproduce, it also appears that they're so resilient that they can last a lifetime and don't necessarily need to do so.

As complex as we appear on the outside, our organs, bones, and other tissues are mostly made up of only four elements: hydrogen, nitrogen, oxygen, and carbon. Ironically, these four elements are among the most abundant materials in the entire universe. We're literally made of the same stuff that makes stars and galaxies. Clearly, when it comes to the building blocks that make up our bodies, there appears to be no shortage of raw materials. So, what *do* we die from?

With the exception of misused medicines and misdiagnosed conditions, the greatest threat to the life of adults over the age of 65 is heart disease. I find this statistic fascinating because of the work that our hearts continuously do. The average human heart beats approximately 100,000 times daily, equaling over 2.5 billion times a year, and pumps 6 quarts of blood through approximately 12,000 miles of arteries, vessels, and capillaries every 24 hours. Our hearts appear to be so vital to who and what we become in life that it's the first organ to form in our mother's womb, even before the brain!

In engineering terms, when the success of an entire project depends upon a single

component, that piece of equipment is given the status of "mission critical." In the space program, for example, when a rover will be landing on Mars and there will be no one around to fix something that might break, the engineers must do one of two things to assure the success of the mission. They either build the one piece of the rover that the whole mission depends upon—*the mission-critical piece*—with such precision that it cannot go wrong, or they build backup systems that can take over if it does. Sometimes they even do both.

Clearly, the miraculous organ that feeds life blood to every cell of our bodies has developed—either by conscious design or natural processes—to be our most self-healing and long-lasting "mission-critical" piece of equipment. Anytime the loss of someone we love is attributed to the "failure" of such a magnificent organ, we must ask ourselves what has *really* happened to that person. Why would the first organ to develop in someone's body, and one that performs *so* impressively for *so* long, with cells that are *so* enduring that they don't even need to reproduce, simply stop working after only a few decades? It makes no sense, unless there's another factor that we haven't considered.

Modern medicine typically attributes heart conditions to an array of physical and lifestyle factors, ranging from cholesterol and diet to environmental toxins and stress. While these factors may be accurate on a purely chemical level, they do little to address the reason "why" they even exist! What does "failure of the heart" really mean?

Perhaps it's not a coincidence that all of the lifestyle factors linked to heart failure are also linked to the unseen force that ancient spiritual traditions describe as the powerful language that speaks to the universe itself: human emotion. Is there something that we *feel* over the course of our lives that, for some of us, can lead to the catastrophic failure of the most important organ in the body?

The Hurt That Kills

The answer to the question of what ends our lives may seem surprising. A growing body of evidence from leading-edge researchers suggests that life itself can lead to the failure of the body! Specifically, it is the unresolved negative emotions—*our hurts*—that have the power to create the physical conditions that we recognize as cardiovascular disease: tension, inflammation, high blood pressure, and clogged arteries. This mind-body relationship was documented recently in a landmark study at Duke University directed by James Blumenthal.[4] He identified long-term experiences of fear, frustration, anxiety, and disappointment as examples of the kind of heightened negative emotions that are destructive to the heart and put us at risk. Each is part of a broader umbrella that we commonly identify as "hurt."

Additional studies support this relationship. Therapist Tim Laurence, founder of the Hoffman Institute in England, describes the potential impact of our failure to heal and forgive what he calls "old hurts and disappointments."

"At the very least," Laurence says, "it cuts you off from good health."[5] He supports this statement by citing a number of studies that show, as did Blumenthal's, that physical conditions of anger and tension can lead to problems that include high blood pressure, headaches, lowered immunity, stomach problems, and, finally, heart attacks.

What Blumenthal's study showed was that teaching people to "tone down" their emotional responses to life situations could prevent heart attacks. This is precisely the point of healing our hurt! The nonphysical forces of the things that hurt us create physical effects that literally have the power to damage us—or even end our lives.

Clearly, this study, along with others, isn't suggesting that it's bad or unhealthy to experience negative emotions in the short term. When we do have these feelings in life, they're indicators—personal gauges—telling us that something has happened that's asking for attention and healing. It's only when we ignore these emotions and they go on for months, years, or a lifetime without being resolved, that they may become a problem.

Could the answer to our question of why we die be that, through the pain of life's disappointments, we've hurt ourselves to death? Commenting on this possibility, Blumenthal's study suggests, "Perhaps when people talk about dying of a broken heart, they are really saying that intense emotional reactions to loss

73

and disappointment can cause a fatal heart attack." In the language of their time, ancient traditions suggest precisely this possibility.

The First 100 Years Are the Toughest

So why does the maximum human age seem to hover around the 100-year mark? Why not 200 or even 500 years? If we're to believe accounts in the Torah and Old Testament texts, many ancient people measured their lives in terms of centuries, rather than the decades that we use today. Adam, for example, is documented as having lived for 930 years, Methuselah for 969 years, and Noah for 950 years.

According to the texts, these men were not simply shriveled husks of their former selves, meagerly surviving and hanging on to the frail thread of life. At advanced ages, they were active and vital, enjoying their families and even starting new ones! And why not? We clearly live in bodies that are built to last. The Torah states that Noah lived for 350 years *after* the Great Flood. If he was 950 years old when he died, this would mean that he was fit and vital enough to build the ark that would ensure the survival of the entire human race when he was 600 years old!

If there was a time when people lived longer and healthier lives, what happened? What changed? Through countless texts, and spiritual traditions that have spanned centuries, we're reminded that we are souls expressing ourselves through bodies. And while they're made of the elements of the universe, it's our souls that bring the bodies to life. *When our souls hurt, our pain is transmitted into our bodies as the spiritual quality of the life force that we feed into each cell.*

75

Is it possible that the 100 years or so that we see as the duration of human life is actually the limit of how long the body can endure unresolved hurt in the soul? Does a century tell us how long we can bear the sadness and disappointments of life before they catch up with us? We can all attest to the pain that comes from watching the people we love, the pets we cherish, and the experiences that we grow attached to disappear from our lives. Could a lifetime of loss, disappointment, and betrayal have the power to disable even our strongest and most durable organ: the heart?

Or maybe our hurt is more ancient and goes even deeper.

In addition to such obvious sources of pain, perhaps there's another one that's less obvious, yet so monumental and universally shared that it's hard for us to even bear thinking about it. Across cultures and societies, creation stories state that to become individual souls in our bodies in this world, we must "break away" from a greater collective soul family. At the same time, one of the deepest universal fears is just that: the fear of being separate and alone.

Perhaps the great hurt that underlies any other is the pain of separation from a greater existence. If this is true, maybe we miss our larger soul family so much that we try to fill the void by re-creating a sense of unity through smaller families here on Earth. It's no wonder, then, that their loss can be so devastating to us. It throws us right back into the pain of the original hurt.

For many people, it's their longing to "hold on" to their families, their relationships, and memories of their past experiences that creates the conditions that lead to their greatest suffering. When they yearn for the things that they can never have again and the people they miss, alcohol and drugs too often become the socially acceptable anesthetics that are used to numb such deep soul pain.

If we can find a way to appreciate the time that we share with those we love, as well as a way to feel good about the time we had when it's over, then we will have taken a giant step toward our greatest healing. From this perspective, the same principles that allow us to hurt ourselves to death also work in reverse. They offer us the healing power of life. This key appears to be related to the way we feel about what life shows us.

While all of these are possibilities to think about, what we know for certain is this: There's a biological potential for our bodies to last much longer, and for us to live healthier and richer lives than we seem to experience at present. In addition to the physical elements of our bodies, there's something that seems to be missing from the modern equation for longevity, however. Regardless of what we choose to call it, that "something" appears to be the spiritual force that feeds our bodies. In the language of another time, the ancients left us instructions for how we may nourish this vital force upon which all life depends.

Their knowledge can empower us to transform past hurt into healing wisdom. To live long, healthy, and vital lives, we must make sense of life's hurts.

We Must _Feel_ to Love

The power of wisdom, beauty, and prayer described by many ancient traditions has been rediscovered through modern experiences. As we saw in the Introduction, for example, the underlying theme in the knowledge of the Navajo is based in recognizing the relationship between the pain in their outer world, and the wisdom and love in their hearts. Although unquestionably different experiences, hurt, wisdom, and love appear to be closely linked through an odd and perhaps unexpected relationship.

Through our hurt, we're shown our capacity to feel—the deeper the hurt, the more powerful the feelings. In our deepest feelings of pain, we discover the depth of our capacity to love. Forgiveness appears to be directly linked to our hurt as well. The greater the hurt, explains Tim Laurence, the greater the benefits

79

of forgiveness. *From this perspective, our hurt may be considered to be a barometer of our ability to love, rather than a punishment for the choices we make.* It is this subtle relationship that demonstrates the force that many traditions describe as the "glue" that holds our world together—the power of our love. We find our greatest healing in our power to love.

It's almost as if we come to this world and test ourselves in ways that are unthinkable to rational and loving people. Through the course of our relationships, jobs, losses, and failures of life, we push ourselves to the very edge of who we believe we are. All the while, we're asking ourselves the same question: "Can we love in the presence of these experiences?" Can we love in the presence of unthinkable atrocities that have been justified by the color of our skin, or how we acknowledge God? Can we love in a world where others have tried to kill the things that they don't understand, and wipe entire peoples from the face of the earth?

Personally, each of us has suffered the loss of loved ones who were here one day and then suddenly disappeared from our lives. We've seen others who suffered from disease in ways that no creature in any world should ever have to endure. When they're gone, we ask ourselves, "Can we love while we hurt from their absence?" Our love is often tested in ways that we would never consciously choose, or could never have imagined. Each time life asks if we can still love, the answer is the same. It's a great big resounding "Yes!" because we're still here.

Whether we call it by the same name or simply live what it means in our lives, it makes no difference—our love is what sustains us. It carries us through the tough times, as well as the great times, and promises that we will always heal from the worst hurts that life can offer. The ancient key to allowing our love to heal us is to let it into our lives. To do so, we must find a way to change our greatest hurts into our deepest wisdom.

81

Turning Hurt into Wisdom

As part of a natural cycle, the experiences of "hurt" and "wisdom" appear to be closely related. While hurt comes from the way we *interpret an experience,* changing the way we feel about what has happened shifts our focus in the cycle. When an experience hurts so much that it's easier to deny it, distract ourselves from it, or in some way avoid dealing with it than it is to address it head on, we may easily find ourselves stuck in our feelings. Within each of us is the power to transmute our hurt, however, into its healed form of wisdom, regardless of where it comes from. While the experience that originally caused the hurt remains unchanged, the way we feel about our suffering is where we find our power.

At first glance, this understanding appears to be asking us to simply go through the motions, faking a new feeling about the events of our lives. A closer investigation, however, reveals that the ancients understood, and applied, an age-old, subtle principle that has been recognized only recently by Western science. That principle suggests that the world around us is a living mirror—the quantum fabric that reflects the emotions that live within us. More specifically, the patterns of health in our bodies, the support of our families, communities, and the peace of our world, tend to mirror our deepest beliefs. This relationship between belief and experience is now firmly supported in the newest theories of 21st-century physics.

It appears that this principle holds true for both the beliefs that we consider "negative" as well as "positive." Life-affirming emotions such as gratitude, compassion, and love are now documented as being triggers for life-promoting conditions such as lower blood pressure, release of "good" hormones, and enhanced immune responses. In a similar fashion, life-denying emotions such as anger, hate, jealousy, and rage are shown to promote life-threatening conditions such as irregular heart rhythms, impaired immune responses, and increased levels of stress hormones.

Perhaps it isn't surprising, then, to discover that within the subtlety of this principle we also find the key to what many believe is the single most powerful force in creation! In the story of his search for truth in life, Gurdjieff found himself in a remote and hidden monastery in an unnamed country, where he was invited to remain until he had awakened a great power within himself. "Stay here," his master said, "until you acquire a force in you that nothing can destroy." I believe that this force was the love, wisdom, and compassion that comes from the healing of hurt. The key that gives new meaning to the things that hurt us is the same key that allows us to move beyond our judgments of life. It is the ancient power of blessing.

Chapter Three

THE THIRD SECRET:
BLESSING IS THE RELEASE

Out beyond ideas of wrongdoing and right-doing, there is a field. I will meet you there.

— Rumi

ANCIENT TRADITIONS SUGGEST THAT THE ONLY DIFFERENCE BETWEEN THE ANGELS OF THE HEAVENS AND THE ANGELS OF THE EARTH IS THAT THE ANGELS OF THE HEAVENS REMEMBER THAT THEY'RE ANGELS. WHEN WE LOVE, WE OFTEN FIND OURSELVES LOVING WITH THE OPENNESS AND INNOCENCE OF AN ANGEL. IT IS THIS SAME OPENNESS THAT ALLOWS OUR PAIN. IT IS *BECAUSE* OF OUR INNOCENCE THAT WE CAN SO DEEPLY FEEL HURT.

If, in fact, we're all angels, then we're very powerful ones. Our anger and rage, as well as our love and compassion, certainly testify to that! These emotions show us how deeply we can feel, and how much positive or negative energy we can direct toward the things that we feel passionately about.

When I see mobs of angry people in the streets of any country killing and destroying the very things that are important to them, I often find myself thinking, *What angry angels!* Regardless of whether you believe that we're angels or not, the reality is that there's something about us that allows us to hurt emotionally in a way that appears to be unparalleled in other creatures. When we do feel hurt, the power of blessing is key to our healing.

Sometimes life challenges the beliefs of even the most loving and saintly people. Commenting on his faith in God following the 2004 tragedy at Beslan's School Number 1, the Archbishop of Canterbury said, "When you see the depth of energy that people can put into such evil, then of course, yes, there is a flicker of doubt. It would be inhuman, I think, not to react that way."[1]

Although we may believe that there are spiritual reasons for the tragedies of our world, we're still left to find a way to make sense of them. Prayer is often the recommended antidote to ease the pain of tragedy. When the great spiritual masters invite us to heal life's hurts through prayer, we must ask the obvious question: How are we to pray "positive" prayers while we're angry and hurt and just want our pain to stop? Understanding how our prayers work offers the answer to precisely this question.

More than 19 centuries before Western scientists acknowledged the field of energy that connects all things, ancient scholars and indigenous healers described the "web of creation" in the words of their day. In the Hopi tradition, for example, the ancient Song of Creation describes a time when the people of the earth will remember that the feminine energy of Spider Woman is the web that unites the universe. The Buddhist sutras tell of a place "far away in the heavenly abode of the great God Indra" where the "wonderful net" that unites us with the universe actually originates.

Clearly, the idea of a unifying force that holds everything together was a common theme. If the ancients knew that the Field exists, is it possible that they also knew how to use it? What secrets did our ancestors know in their time that we've forgotten in ours? Preserved in texts, traditions, and temple walls, those who came before us left behind nothing less than the description of a quantum principle that we're only beginning to understand today. With that description, we've been given the exact instructions we need to bring the "beautiful and wild forces" of prayer described by St. Francis into our lives. The key is found in a place that may surprise you!

The Mystery of the Space Between

There's a power that lives in the space "between," that subtle instant when something ends and what follows next hasn't yet begun. From the birth and death of galaxies, to the beginning and ending of careers and relationships, and even in the simplicity of breathing in and out, creation is the story of beginnings and endings: cycles that start and stop, expand and contract, live and die.

Regardless of scale, between the "beginning" and the "end," there exists a moment in time when neither one has fully happened. That moment is where magic and miracles come from! In the instant of between, all possibilities exist and none have been chosen. From this place, we're given the power to heal our bodies, change our lives, and bring peace to the world. All events originate from this powerful, magical moment.

91

The mystery and possibilities of the space that connects two events has long been honored in the wisdom traditions of our past. Native traditions of North America, for example, state that two times each day the earth enters into precisely such mystical realms. We find one realm immediately *after* the sun disappears below the horizon, just *before* the darkness of night arrives. The second realm occurs just *before* the sun reappears from the edge of the sky, *after* the darkest part of the night.

Both are twilight moments—neither completely day nor completely night. It is during this time, the traditions suggest, that an opening occurs in which profound truths may be realized, deep healings may occur, and prayers have their greatest power. In his classic work *A Separate Reality,* anthropologist Carlos Castaneda called this opening a "crack between the worlds," and described it as an access point into the unseen realms of spirits, demons, and power.

Modern scientists acknowledge the power of just such a place. For them, however, the point is less about day, night, and time, and more about the matter that our world is made of. From the perspective of a scientist, what we see as the solid world around us is anything but solid!

When the local movie theater projects a moving image on the screen in front of us, for example, we know that the story we're seeing is an illusion. The romance and tragedy that tugs at our heartstrings is actually the result of many still pictures being flashed very rapidly, one after another, to create the *sense* of a continuous story. While our eyes do see the single pictures, frame by frame, our brain merges them together into what we perceive as that uninterrupted film.

Quantum physicists suggest that our world works in much the same way. For instance, what we see as the football touchdown or triple axel of a figure skater on a Sunday-afternoon sports program, in quantum terms, is actually a series of individual events that happen very quickly and closely together. Similar to the way in which many images strung together make a movie look so real, life actually occurs as brief, tiny bursts of light called *quanta*. The quanta of life happen so quickly that, unless our brain is trained to operate differently (as it would in some forms of meditation), it simply averages the pulses to create the continuous action we see as the Sunday sports.

Within this simplified explanation of life, we also find the key to our healing. For one burst of light to end before the next begins, there must, by definition, be a moment in between. Within this space, for a brief instant, there exists a perfect balance where nothing is happening— the events that led to the burst are complete, and the new events haven't started. In this place of "no thing," all scenarios of life/death/suffering/healing/war/peace exist as possibilities and

93

potential. This is the place where feelings and prayers become the blueprints of life.

The key is that our emotional state *during* prayer determines the kind of blueprint we create. Knowing that the Field is a reflection of our inner beliefs, we must find a way to clear our hurt and anger *before* we pray. If we think about this, it makes tremendous sense. After all, how could we expect the Mind of God to reflect healing and peace if we're feeling fear and hurt?

So, in the presence of the powerful emotions of anger, frustration, jealousy, and hurt, how are we to feel something else so that our prayers have their greatest power? How do we suspend our "negative" emotions while we access the powerful space between? To answer this question, once again we turn to the wisdom of our past.

Rumi's Field: Beyond Judgment

There's no doubt as to the power that the ancient authors of the Dead Sea Scrolls attributed to the space between. In *The Essene*

Gospel of Peace, we're reminded, "In the moment between the breathing in, and the breathing out, is hidden all the mysteries . . ." As in other traditions, in the highest orders of Essene teachings we are left instructions on how to use the space between to prepare ourselves for prayer.

Specifically, they describe how we might prepare our minds, hearts, and bodies *before* the prayer ever begins. Even if it's for only a moment, we're invited to create an experience that temporarily suspends our judgments, fears, and hurts. From this neutral state, we may offer our prayer from strength and clarity, rather than from the clouded judgment that stems from hurt. This allows us to enter into our sacred dialogue with the Mind of God in a state of consciousness that brings the greatest benefit of prayer to our lives.

Through words that are both eloquent and simple, the Sufi poet Rumi invites us to join him in this neutral place once we've discovered it within ourselves. He shares his invitation in two brief yet powerful statements:

"Out beyond ideas of wrongdoing and right-doing, there is a field. I will meet you there."[2]

How do we get to this place when life shows us a world that appears to be scary and dangerous? The instructions are precise.

Blessing: The Emotional Lubricant

Today we find the key to Rumi's field beyond wrongdoing and rightdoing in the wisdom of blessing. Perhaps contrary to the popular belief that when we bless something we put our stamp of approval on it, this form of blessing doesn't condone, discourage, or encourage any action, circumstance, or event. It doesn't agree or disagree with any point of view. It simply acknowledges what has occurred. The act of acknowledgment without judgment is the opening that allows healing to begin.

Here's the reason why: When we see something that hurts us so badly that we need to react, shut down, or turn away, our tendency is to disregard what we feel. This is how we cope with many experiences. We shut off the emotion surrounding what we've experienced and hide it somewhere deep inside to keep it from hurting us even more. But the hurt doesn't just "go away." It goes wherever we store it.

97

Then, at a time when we least expect, it finds a way to reemerge, often in a form that we would never choose. This is especially common in people who've experienced emotionally traumatic scenes ranging from battlefield conditions and rape to childhood abuse and domestic violence.

The disproportionate anger that may surface during such moments can often be traced back to the shock of an experience earlier in life that couldn't be dealt with when it happened. In these cases, a seemingly innocent and off-the-cuff comment from a significant other or co-worker can become the trigger that awakens the earlier hurt.

Our ability to "shut down" is the defense mechanism that allows us to go on with life, and not have to deal with the immediate pain of something that shocks our senses and sensibilities. At the same time, the emotions that have been created within us are still there, although they're buried. Tim Laurence views the acknowledgment of hurt as an uncomfortable yet necessary step in healing. "It is a process of emotional catharsis," he states, "which enables people to get over that feeling of being wronged."[3]

Some people may find the defense mechanism of disguising their hurt works so well, in fact, that they believe they've healed the experience. They may even believe that they've forgotten what it was that hurt them in the first place. Their bodies, however, don't forget. Studies have shown that DNA and the cells of our bodies are in direct communication with the feelings that we have regarding our lives. For each feeling, the body creates a matching chemistry. Through the release of life-affirming hormones, such as DHEA, or life-denying hormones such as cortisol, we literally experience what may be called "love" chemistry and "hate" chemistry.

99

Intuitively, we know this to be true, because we know that joy and appreciation have a positive influence upon our bodies, making us feel energized and lighter, while anger and fear have the opposite effect. Some holistic traditions even suggest that diseases such as cancer are expressions of unresolved anger, hurt, and guilt emerging from parts of the body where they were stored years earlier. Although we may not be able to prove this scientifically at the moment, the correlation between emotional trauma and the organs associated with the trauma clearly exists and deserves more study. With these understandings in mind, it appears that to disregard the things that hurt us may have long-term effects that aren't in our best interests.

It makes sense to find a way to transform anything that has hurt us into a new experience that helps us. We can do this by acknowledging it, and allowing it to move *through* the body. This is where the act of blessing enters the healing process.

100 *Blessing Defined*

Blessing may be defined as a quality of thought/feeling/emotion that allows us to redefine our feelings about something that's hurting us now or has hurt us in the past. Stated another way, blessing something is the "lubricant" that frees our hurtful emotions, opening us up to greater healing, rather than keeping our emotions stuck and unresolved within the body. To lubricate our emotions, we must acknowledge (bless) all aspects of those hurtful things: such as those who suffer, the cause of the suffering, and those who witness the outcome.

I often find at this point in any discussion of what blessing *is* that it's important to be very clear about what it *is not*. When we bless someone who's hurt us, clearly we aren't suggesting that what has happened is okay or that we'd like it to happen again. Blessing doesn't condone or make excuses for any atrocity or act of suffering. It doesn't put a stamp of approval on a hurtful event, or suggest that we would ever choose to reexperience it.

What blessing *does do* is free us from our painful experiences. It acknowledges that those events, whatever they were, have occurred. When we do so, our feelings about those experiences move *through* our bodies instead of getting stuck inside them. In this way, blessing is the key to reaching Rumi's field beyond wrongdoing and rightdoing. Blessing is the key to accessing the space between. It temporarily suspends our hurt long enough so that we can replace it with another feeling.

Through the act of blessing, you assume your power to release life's deepest hurts and unresolved feelings. Blessing does so without the need to trace those feelings back to their

101

origins, relive the pain again and again to get to the bottom of it, or embark upon the endless search to understand why things happened in the way they did. While all of these paths may work to some degree, and for some people, without the need for any ability other than what you already have inside of you, the single act of blessing gives you the power to change your life. And it does so in a heartbeat! When we can make our choices and offer our prayers from a place of strength and clarity, rather than from the weakness of rage and hurt, something wonderful begins to happen.

102

Sound too simple to work? Such a powerful tool can be as simple or as difficult as we choose to make it. The reason that blessing works so well is easy to understand. It's impossible to judge something while we're blessing it at the same time. Our minds won't allow us to do both things at once.

I invite you to try the blessing process by following the instructions on the next few pages. Think of a person, place, or experience that has hurt you in the past, and then apply the process. You may be surprised by the power, effectiveness, and simplicity in the ancient secret of blessing.

Before You Can Bless . . .

There is one prerequisite before you can do a blessing, however. To prepare for accepting the blessing into your life, you must first truthfully and honestly answer a single question. It isn't necessary for you to do this formally or in front of another person unless you're more comfortable doing so. This question is for you alone, and it will help you know even better where your conditioning is with regard to the "rights" and "wrongs" of your life.

The question is this: "Am I ready to move beyond a 'gut' reaction or an old belief that 'someone must pay' or 'I need to get even' in order to right a wrong?" In other words, are you ready to move beyond the type of thinking that justifies hurting someone because they've hurt you?

If you answer *yes* to this question, then the blessing is for you, and you're going to like the results you experience! If your answer is *no,* then your path is to find out *why* you would choose to hold on to a belief that keeps you locked into the hurt that leads to the very suffering you're trying to heal.

In the tradition of blessing, clearly there are no right or wrong answers to these questions. They are merely designed to help you be very clear about where you are in your thought processes and what you hope to achieve through your beliefs.

The Ancient Key

While the act of blessing may appear to be in direct conflict with the beliefs of some traditions, it is also closely aligned with the teachings of some of the great spiritual masters of the past. I offer it here because I've personally found that it holds the key to the greatest depth of healing, for the greatest number of people, in the shortest amount of time.

The Western spiritual texts preserving much of the wisdom of blessing were either edited, or in some cases, completely deleted. Today, we're left to glean ancient techniques preserved in the "lost" biblical books that were recovered in the mid-20th century. Interestingly, one of the best descriptions of the power of nonjudgment is also among the most controversial: the Gospel of Thomas, which was discovered as part of the Nag Hammadi Library.

The crux of this portion of the Gospels is a record of things that Jesus said to those he knew during his lifetime. It's here that we find an account of a conversation he had with his disciples regarding the secrets of life, death, and immortality. In response to a question about what we can look forward to as our eventual fate, Jesus begins by offering keys into what he calls "trees" of our existence, attributes of life that are constant and enduring. "Whoever becomes acquainted with them [the trees] will not experience death,"[4] he suggests. One of these keys is the ability to remove ourselves from judgment.

In the familiar elegance that we often find in true wisdom, Jesus describes the state of neutral consciousness by telling the disciples what they must do to enter the place of immortality that he calls "the kingdom."

"When you make the two one," he begins, "and when you make the inside like the outside, and the outside like the inside, and the above like the below, and when you make the male and the female one in the same . . . then you will enter the kingdom." [5] Very quickly we get the idea of what he's saying.

It's only when we can see *beyond* the differences that we judge—that is, when we dissolve the polarities that have made things separate in the past—that we create for ourselves the state of being where we "will not experience death." When we can move beyond the right and the wrong, the good and the bad of what life shows us, then we find our greatest power to become more than the things that have hurt us. Although our minds know that these things may exist on one level, *it's the feeling in our hearts* that speaks to the Field of the Mind of God . . . and creates.

107

As both a teacher and a healer, in this way Jesus has shown us how to transcend our hurts through the wisdom of our hearts. While other teachings suggest similar techniques, those described by Jesus are perhaps the clearest and most concise. This may be due, in part, to the lessons that he learned during his apprenticeship with other spiritual traditions. While Thomas offers us the essence of Jesus' teachings, in modern translations of his gospel we're left feeling a little like we may be reading the *Reader's Digest* condensed version of ideas that could go much further!

Following is an expanded explanation of how Jesus' blessing process works, taken as a composite from his teachings, as well as a number of additional ones.

The Instructions

In Western translations of the Bible, we're simply told to "bless" with very little insight into how to bless, or why the practice works. Perhaps the best known of these references are the familiar passages where Jesus describes to his disciples the spiritual qualities that will best serve them in this world and the next. "Bless them that curse you, and pray for them which despitefully use you."[6] As strange as these words may sound in today's world where it's easy to confuse justice with "getting even," I can only imagine how foreign this way of thinking was 2,000 years ago!

In the edited translations, we see this theme continue in varying degrees throughout Jesus' teachings. In the biblical book of Romans, for example, the instructions regarding how we may respond to harassment leaves little doubt in our minds as to the intent of the message. "Bless them which persecute you; bless, and curse not."[7]

Although many of Jesus' teachings on the subject of blessing were offered to deal with personal attacks, either verbal or physical, the idea of blessing also extends to the pain we feel from knowing that others are being hurt.

When we experience something that is hurtful to us, there are three places where emotional pain may appear. While some of these are obviously easier to address than others, all three must be acknowledged for the blessing to work. This is the power of blessing: It elevates us beyond the ancient trap of the rightness and wrongness of what has happened.

"Why," you may ask, "would I ever want to bless the very things that have hurt me?" This is a great question, and one that I asked years ago when I discovered the power of blessing for myself. The answer is clear, and even deceptively simple. We have two choices regarding how we deal with life's hurts: Either we may mask and bury them, and allow them to slowly steal from us the very things that we cherish until they eventually destroy us, or we may accept the healing that comes from acknowledging life's hurts, and move forward with healthy, vital lives. I personally believe that this is the intent of the statement found in the Gospel of Thomas that reads: "If you bring forth that which you have within you, it will save you. If you do not, it will destroy you."

The challenge, as well as the reward, for applying this principle in our lives may best be summed up in the words of St. Francis. He says of his lifetime, "It was easy to love God in all that was beautiful. The lessons of deeper knowledge, though, instructed me to embrace God in all things." This means the ugly experiences as well as the beautiful ones. The choice is ours. If we choose the healing, blessing is the path.

When we do choose to bless in our lives, there are typically three aspects or groups of people in each situation that ask to be blessed. Although there are always exceptions, more often than not we must bless those who suffer, the cause of the suffering, and those who witness and are left behind. Each of these is described briefly as follows:

Blessing Those Who Suffer: The first place to direct our blessing is toward the obvious suffering of those who are hurt. In some

110

cases, such as the September 11 and Beslan tragedies, there may be a distance between us and those who are suffering from an almost unimaginable magnitude of loss. In other instances, such as a broken promise or betrayal of trust from a loved one, the suffering may be right in our own backyard, as *we're the ones* who are suffering. In any case, this is perhaps the easiest part of the blessing process, blessing those who are the object of the suffering.

Blessing Whatever Causes the Suffering: For many people, this is the hardest part. For others, however, blessing the people or things that inflict the hurt, cause us pain, and take from us the parts of ourselves that we cherish the most is so aligned with the traditions with which we've grown up that we find it's almost second nature.

This is where the power of the blessing becomes very real in our lives. When we can find it within ourselves to bless the people and things that hurt us, we become new. It takes a strong person to rise above the rights and the wrongs of events, and say, "Today, I am more than the hurt of my past."

I've met people who tell me, "I will do this 'blessing thing' only one time, when no one else is around, because my friends would never

111

understand this way of thinking. And if I don't like what happens," they continue, "I'll go back to feeling the hatred and jealousy that's worked for me in the past."

I reply, "Great! One time is all it takes!" I feel confident in my response for one reason alone. The moment—*the instant*—that we open the door to a greater possibility of blessing in our lives, we change inside. There's a shift. In that change, we can never go back . . . and why would we want to? Why would we ever *choose* to feel the feelings that hurt us in the long run if we can feel the feelings that heal us instead?

Whether you try it once and go back—or not—you must address all aspects of the experience for the blessing to work, including blessing the people, places, and things that you most dislike and may have the greatest anger toward.

Blessing Those Who Witness the Suffering: This is the part of the blessing that's so easy to overlook. In addition to the relationship between those who suffer and those who cause the suffering, there are those who are left to make sense of what remains. It is us! We who

are left behind must reconcile the murder of civilians and innocent children in times of war, the brutality against women in many societies, and the aftermath of failed relationships and broken homes.

While it's easy to forget about ourselves in the presence of another's hurt, it's also our reaction—*our lingering feelings*—that form the message we're sending into the Mind of God following any tragedy. Ultimately, it's how we feel as individuals as well as collectively that fills the void in consciousness following any tragedy, on any scale, from family to global. Bless us in our witnessing!

The Blessing Template

The key to receiving the gift of blessing is that it must be offered.

First, find a place of privacy, where no one will hear what you're about to do. Then, simply begin by stating the following out loud:

- "I bless _____."
  [Place here the name(s) of those who are suffering or have suffered.]

- "I bless _____."
  [Place here the name(s) of who or
  what has inflicted the suffering. It
  helps to be as specific as possible.]

- "I bless me in the witnessing."

Keep on Blessing!

My experience of using the blessing tem-
plate above is that it sometimes takes a time
or two before it really works. The reason for
this isn't unexpected. To survive in this world,
we've all learned to lock our hurts skillfully
away within ourselves. Sometimes we do such
a good job of masking our feelings about our
experiences that *even we* forget where we've
hidden them. Please don't be disappointed if it
seems as if your blessing isn't working the first
few times that you use it. It may take a couple
of repetitions to penetrate the shell that you
made to protect yourself.

So keep on blessing. Say your blessing out
loud. Then say it again. And again. Use direct
names, organizations, people, and dates each
time you identify those who have caused the

115

pain that you're blessing. The more specific you are, the clearer the access you create to your body's memory of the hurt. Repeat your blessing until you feel warmth in your body that extends outward from the pit of your stomach. As you continue, that warmth will rise and expand throughout your body.

Don't be surprised if you find yourself welling up with tears and sobbing huge sobs. This is the way that the blessing frees our hurt and enables it to move through us. When the blessing feels complete, the world feels different. Although the reason for our hurt still exists, what has happened is that we've changed the way *we feel* about our hurt. This is the power of the blessing. This is also the place where words may fail you—it simply becomes something that you have to experience for yourself to understand.

I know people who have found the power of blessing and now bless everything in sight! From the bodies of flattened animals that are just "sleeping" on the side of the road, to each news event that flashes across the television screen, they offer a blessing just under their breath many times each day. When these people ride in my car and we pass an ambulance either going to or from the hospital, or even when someone recklessly drives past us in a no-passing zone on a narrow mountain road, their blessings are second nature. It's as automatic as saying "Bless you" when someone sneezes. Don't be surprised if you find that "random acts of blessing" begin to appear spontaneously in your life as well!

In our last section, I asked the question of how we can pray positive prayers while we're still experiencing negative emotions such as hurt, anger, hate, and the desire for revenge. One of the secrets of the wisdom traditions is that our prayers are most effective when we pre-pare ourselves as a whole being—mind, body, and spirit—to enter into a sacred conversation with the Mind of God. If the Field is going to reflect back to us what we've become, then it becomes more important than ever for us to be in what Native Americans call "a good place" when we pray for healing from our hurt.

The ancient gift of blessing paves the way for us to pray from a place of strength and clarity, rather than weakness and uncer-tainty. While the instructions may be useful and interesting, I find that wisdom teachings are sometimes best shared as stories. The more real the story, the more the example makes sense. The following story describes my first experience with blessing during a time of personal loss. Although it may pale in comparison to the really "big" hurts in our world, at the time that it happened blessing is what helped me deal with the loss of a dear friend. This example may help you deal with your losses, too.

Blessing in Loss

Some of my most compelling relationships have been with animals. One week in the early 1990s, I was leading a combination workshop and retreat at an inn in Mount Shasta, California. A tiny black kitten wandered down the hallways of the inn, found his way into my room and my heart, and never left.

My newfound friend had been born about five weeks earlier to a young female cat that had never given birth before and could not nurse her litter. By the time the employees at the inn discovered what had happened, they believed that all of the kittens had died. A few days later, however, a small miracle occurred. The mother cat emerged from her hiding place carrying a tiny heap of bones and fur that had survived all that time without food! Immediately the staff began to nurse the tiny kitten back to health. Acknowledging his magical strength and sheer will to survive, they named him Merlin.

Finding my room that evening, Merlin purred and meowed at the door until I gave in to my urge to care for every animal on the entire planet and let him in. During the week of the program, he slept with me each night and sat with me each morning as I ate breakfast in my room. He would watch me shave from the edge of the bathroom sink and walk across my 35-millimeter slides (in the days *before* PowerPoint!) as I prepared them for the next day. Every morning he would stand on the edge of the bathtub as I showered, and catch droplets of water in his mouth as they bounced from my body. By the end of the week, Merlin and I were good friends, and I found myself tremendously attached to the little miracle with such a will to live.

Through a series of synchronicities that soon occurred, Merlin and I found ourselves on a cross-country journey to my home in the high desert of northern New Mexico. He quickly became my "family," and for the next

119

three years he was with me each evening while I prepared dinner, and he napped beside my ancient Apple computer while I wrote my first book.

One night Merlin went outside, as he always did at that time of evening, and I never saw him again. It was in the summer of 1994, during the week that a massive comet was impacting Jupiter. At first I thought that maybe he'd just gone exploring, as cats sometimes do, and I'd see him again soon. It may have been that Merlin navigated through the desert using the magnetic lines of the earth, as birds and whales do—the same fields that were upset by Jupiter's strange effect on earth's magnetic fields. These could have shifted and led him somewhere else. Or it may have been for a host of other reasons. The fact was that Merlin was gone.

121

When I didn't see him after two days, I began to search for him. I took no phone calls and did absolutely no business for nearly a week as I scoured the fields north of Taos, New Mexico. Was he caught in a trap that the ranchers had set for the coyotes that hunted their sheep? Maybe he was stuck in an old building or a well and couldn't get out. For days I searched owls' nests and looked in every badger burrow and coyote den that I could find. Finally, I stopped looking for Merlin and began looking for traces of him: his fur or his collar. All my efforts were fruitless.

One morning as I was lying in bed just before sunrise in a dreamy half-awakened state, I simply asked for a sign. I needed to know what had happened to my friend. Before I'd even finished the question in my mind, something happened that had never happened before and has never happened since. From the loft in my home, I heard a sound coming from outside, then another, and then another. Within seconds, coming from every direction, completely encircling the property, I heard the unmistakable cry of coyotes—more than I'd ever heard in all the years that I'd lived on that property.

For what seemed like minutes, they yipped and howled until just as suddenly as they began, they stopped. I had tears in my eyes as I said out loud, "I don't think Merlin is with me any longer." In that moment, I was shown what had happened to my friend. I knew that the coyotes had taken him, and that I would never see him again.

Later the same day, I began to see coyotes all over the property—in broad daylight! Certainly I'd seen them in the past, yet always before, they'd appeared at sunset or just before sunrise. Today, they were everywhere in the middle of the afternoon—single ones, two or three together, young pups and families, all casually strolling through the fields.

Here is the reason that I offer this story. The loss of Merlin hurt me. In my hurt, I could have gone after each coyote, one by one, thinking that "this is the one" that took my friend. I could have stood high on the top of a farm building with a rifle in my hands and avenged Merlin's death until there were no coyotes left in the entire valley. I could have done all that . . . and nothing would have changed. Merlin would still be gone. I wasn't angry at the coyotes; I just missed my friend. I missed his personality and the funny sounds that he made as he stalked "big game" like the moths on the screen door at night. I missed the way he looked at me upside down while lying on the cool tile floors in the summer.

That afternoon I began driving along the dusty gravel road that weaves its way through the valley to the highway. It was on this drive

123

that I had my first experience of blessing. As I rolled up the windows so no one would hear me (not that there was anyone within miles of me anyway!), I blessed Merlin in his passing, acknowledging him and all of the joy that he brought to my life. That was the easy part. Then I began to bless the coyotes, especially the ones that took his life. Before long, I actually began to feel an odd sort of kinship with them. I knew that what had happened was not an intentional act to hurt me. They simply did what coyotes do! I blessed myself in trying to make sense of why nature sometimes seems so cruel.

124

At first nothing seemed to happen. I was so hurt that I couldn't let the blessing "in." Within a couple of repetitions, however, the change began. The feeling started as warmth in my stomach that swelled as it spread throughout my body in all directions. As my eyes welled with tears, I found myself gasping big sobs. I pulled to the side of the road and did my best to bless until there was no energy to bless anymore. I knew, for that day, that the blessing was complete.

The thing about the act of blessing is that the world doesn't change; it's only we who change! In our willingness to acknowledge and release whatever it is that has hurt us, the world looks different and we become stronger, healthier people.

Interestingly, following the peace that I made with the coyotes that day, although I hear them at night, I've never seen another one cross our property line. Last year, however, I did see another cat of a different kind: my very first live mountain lion. And she'd crossed under the fence line to come right into my backyard!

125

When Turning Away Isn't Enough

While the story of Merlin may seem like an insignificant example, I offer it because it's real and deeply personal. The principle of blessing that I described for Merlin works for any hurt that you may experience, from the local to the global. I recently had the opportunity to put the power of blessing to the test in the face of one of the most disturbing and horrifying acts that I've experienced as an adult. Just as before, it was the key that allowed me to keep my faith in the world, and gave me the strength to vow that we leave this world a better place than the one we find ourselves living in today.

I felt my body tighten in response to what I'd heard. An American civilian working in Iraq had just been executed—his head severed from his body—and dumped at the side of a road without any of the dignity or respect that is due to human life anywhere in the world.

I was in Europe on a book tour when CNN International reported the brutal killing. The news anchor stated that, although news agencies in other parts of the world were showing the video and photographs to document the slaying, CNN had chosen not to. In place of the actual images, however, the commentator offered a detailed account of what *he* had seen in the video. As a very visual person, for me this choice was perhaps even worse than seeing the photos themselves. As I heard his verbal description of the last seconds of the man's life, the images that were created in my mind left me deeply disturbed with the unreal feeling that often accompanies news that's a shock to our sensibilities.

One of the lessons that I've learned from the brutal executions in Iraq, as well as the images that document war from any era in history, is that the suffering and intentional loss of life can never really be "understood" in the dictionary sense of the word. It's meaningless for rational and loving people to even try to make sense of the atrocities that accompany such acts of war. To do so, we would have to put ourselves in the place of those in battle, and to think the way they do. At the same time, these events have become part of our world. They are a reality that has happened.

When I've asked audience members how many people have changed their habits of watching news broadcasts, the show of hands tells the story. Without exception, in every audience there are more and more people who claim to watch the news less, or have stopped watching it altogether. In answer to my next question of why, they say that it's simply too depressing and too painful. They no longer want themselves and their families to be bombarded with images of cruelty and suffering, and the feeling that there's nothing they can do to change things.

127

While avoiding the daily onslaught of network terror updates may provide a temporary reprieve, it is short-lived at best. Believe me, I've tried! I found that while it was easy to immerse myself in the daily routines of rural life in a small community, it all catches up with us in one way or another. The events of the world continue. At some point in time, the "big" news items come rushing in as "Have you heard . . . ?" Through word of mouth, a magazine article, or a newspaper headline, we're suddenly left to deal with the very situations that we'd hoped to avoid.

When we find ourselves in such situations, what can we do? Simply looking away isn't the answer. While we may not be able to change what life has shown us, we must find out where it "fits" in order to go on with our own lives.

Whether we feel the hurt of the world or the pain that comes from losing the little things that we cherish in life, the power of blessing works in the same way. My greatest experiences of blessing have come during times of loss. From the sudden death of my father and our unresolved relationship, to the ending of two marriages and the betrayal of trust by those closest to me, I can share the blessing process from a place of conviction, because I know it works.

My prayer is that it works for you as well, and becomes a friend in times of need.

Chapter Four

THE FOURTH SECRET:
BEAUTY IS THE TRANSFORMER

*Beauty is eternity gazing at itself in
a mirror. But you are eternity and
you are the mirror.*

— Kahlil Gibran

BEAUTY MAY BE ONE OF THE LEAST UNDERSTOOD,
YET MOST POWERFUL, OF HUMAN EXPERIENCES.
FROM THE BEGINNING OF RECORDED HISTORY,
WE'VE ENGAGED IN A LONG, STRANGE, AND SOME-
TIMES DANGEROUS DANCE WITH THIS MYSTERIOUS
FORCE. ANCIENT ACCOUNTS OF OUR MOST CHER-
ISHED TRADITIONS ATTRIBUTE THE DOWNFALL OF
POWERFUL ANGELS IN HEAVEN TO THEIR INABIL-
ITY TO RESIST THE BEAUTY OF THE NEWLY CRE-
ATED WOMEN OF OUR SPECIES, THE "DAUGHTERS
OF MAN."

In the biblical book of Enoch the prophet, a cornerstone of the early Christian church, Enoch goes so far as to disclose the identity of the "chief" angels who led the 200 others who couldn't resist the beauty of earthly women.[1] With names such as Samyaza, Ramuel, and Turel, these "perfects" knew that their cohabitation with mortal women violated the rules of the cosmos. Yet for them, the sensual experience that awaited them outweighed the risk of losing their immortality. In later biblical traditions, it was the beauty of one woman, Delilah, which led to the love, trust, betrayal, and eventual death of Samson, one of the most powerful men on Earth.

History is the story of our relationship with beauty: its power and allure, the lengths that we've gone to pursue it, our longing to achieve it, our attempts to capture it, and our belief that we can somehow master it. All the while, we've been hard-pressed to define this most elusive quality of human experience. Precisely what is beauty?

The Mystery of Beauty

Beauty holds different meanings for different people. When people are asked to define it, more often than not their response is based on their personal experience—what it has meant to them in their lives. To a scientist, beauty may come in the form of an elegant solution to a mathematical equation. A photographer, on the other hand, may see beauty in the striking contrast between sunlight and shadows in a composition. Albert Einstein saw beauty as an expression of a greater order in creation, stating, for example, "Mozart's music is so pure and beautiful that I see it as a reflection of the inner beauty of the universe."

It is clear that every person's experience of beauty is unique. For this reason, there may be as many definitions for the experience of beauty as there are people who experience it! Regardless of how it's defined in our lives— whether it's viewed as a force, an experience, a quality, a judgment, or a perception—the

133

power of beauty is real. In its presence, we are changed. While it's clear that we may not know precisely *what* it is, it's equally clear that we may apply what we *do* know about the power of beauty to heal the suffering, hurt, and fear in our lives.

If, as ancient traditions proclaimed, beauty is a force unto itself, it is perhaps the strangest of nature's forces. Unlike gravity and electromagnetism, which seem to exist with or without us, the power of beauty appears to be dormant until we give it our attention. While it may very well have the power to change our world, that power is asleep until it's awakened. And we are the only ones who can awaken it! As the only form of life with the power to experience beauty, it is awakened only when we acknowledge it in our lives.

From this perspective, beauty is more than the things that are pleasing to our eyes. It is an *experience* of heart, mind, and soul. Beauty comes from our willingness to see the perfection in what we often call the "imperfections" of life. While the betrayal of a confidence, for example, may shock us initially, some of that shock may disappear when we consider that we, in turn, have betrayed others in different ways,

134

at other times. The "beauty" in this instance is in the balance of such experiences coming back to us, sometimes in ways we would least expect.

To find the beauty in each experience, perhaps our role is less about creating it and more about recognizing that it's already here. Beauty is always present in all things. It may be found even in places where we believe that beauty could never exist.

In the moments that we reach into the depths of our souls for the power to give new meaning to things that hurt us the most, we discover the great wisdom shared by ancient masters. That wisdom simply reminds us that the power to see beauty is a choice. The choice before us in each moment of every day is to consider only what we're shown in the moment, on its own merits, without comparing one experience to another. This is how we plant the seeds in our awareness that become the attractors inviting greater beauty into our lives.

It is only when we compare our actual experience to an idea of what we believe beauty *should* look like that we're capable of seeing anything other than the beauty of the moment.

In the Navajo tradition, we're reminded of this principle in the simple phrase: "The beauty upon which you base your life."[2] We each create our own standard by which we measure the beauty in our lives. The question is, what do you use as the gauge by which you measure balance, success, and failure in your life? What is your yardstick for beauty?

Beauty Lives Where We Allow It!

At first it was barely noticeable. Standing with our group in an open plaza of Kathmandu's historic district, I had grown accustomed to the bumps and nudges that accompany touring with others in close quarters. To help accustom our bodies to the higher elevations of Tibet, we had scheduled a 48-hour layover in the country of Nepal, which is situated at about 4,000 feet above sea level. In addition to preparing us for the Tibetan plateau, this would give us time to immerse ourselves in the traditions surrounding Hindu's oldest temples. I could have easily ignored the tug that I felt from the cloth pleat in my cotton hiking pants. Because it was so deliberate, though, I did not.

Instinctively, I glanced downward to the source of the distraction. I wasn't prepared for what I saw. My eyes were met by the intense gaze of a man whose sparsely bearded face rose barely above the height of my knees. He appeared both timeless and ancient, as the hot wind rippled through the long, tangled strands of hair that mingled with the silvery wisps of his beard. The white ash that traditionally covers the body of a Hindu holy man clung to the humid dampness of his skin in patches. Underneath was a black, scarred, and deformed body, made only darker from years of exposure to the harsh high-altitude sun.

It took a moment for me to make sense of what my eyes were seeing. As I searched below his waist to the place where the man's legs *should* have been, all that I saw was the limp fold of a soiled loincloth cascading onto the ground below. In place of his legs, there was a short piece of board with rollers attached to the underside. Stained through years of use, the roller board appeared to be his only means of getting around.

Startled, I stepped back. Without breaking his gaze from my eyes, the man slowly placed both of his palms on the ground, maintained his balance on the board, and skillfully pushed himself in my direction. I glanced up to see if anyone else had noticed what I was seeing. Those around me appeared absolutely oblivious to what was happening on the ground beneath their feet!

The sight of overwhelming poverty had become common through the course of our journey, and my immediate assumption was that the man was a "beggar" asking me for a handout. The act of begging is an acceptable profession in many religious traditions for those people who have freed themselves from the encumbrances of homes, professions, and families to devote themselves to prayer. As I reached into my pocket for something to hand him, the man turned and pointed to the roofline of an ancient temple across the square.

Following his gesture, I found myself staring at the most beautiful wooden façade of an ancient Hindu temple. It was partially hidden behind other buildings, and was completely covered with the intricately detailed figurines of the thousands of gods and goddesses of Hindu tradition. If the ashen man had not pointed it out, I would have missed it completely. As I

later learned, it also held an important key to understanding the Hindu faith.

When I handed the bills to him, he casually waved his hands as if he were shooing a fly away, gesturing for me to put the money back into my pocket—he wasn't interested in money! I turned away briefly, in time to catch our translator leading the group in another direction. When I looked back, the man on the roller board had disappeared. Searching the crowd in front of me, I caught a quick glimpse of him just as he made his way across the hot cobblestones and into the masses of tourists. I never saw him again.

140

I share this story to illustrate a point. Because the man looked so very different to me, I had a judgment about him and who he was. From his gnarled and weathered body, it was the beauty of his spirit that came through that day. Rather than wanting a handout, he simply wanted to share something with me. He showed me a part of his world that I would not have seen otherwise, and in doing so he taught me about my judgment. He also demonstrated that beauty can come through only when we allow it.

It's interesting how the universe brings lessons to us when we least expect them! Often, it seems that they come just after we've had a powerful experience, as if to test us to see if we really learned it! This was the case in Tibet.

A few days after my experience in Kathmandu, our bus pulled into a mountain village and stopped at an old military barracks that had been converted into a traveler's lodge. A hunched-over, weathered-looking man boarded our bus as we stopped, and caught everyone a little off guard. As he looked at us, we could see that he was old, had only a couple of teeth, and his eyes were severely crossed, making it difficult to establish eye contact. At first we thought that he might have been another beggar from the street. But when someone in the group offered him some Chinese yuan (local currency), he refused. Instead, he began to take the heaviest bags from inside of our bus so that we wouldn't have to deal with them.

After he had neatly stacked the last bag on the curb in front of the inn, I found myself *wanting* to give him a gratuity. He'd certainly earned it! Our bags seemed to get bigger and heavier with each city we visited. Again, he refused. As he looked up, he grinned a big, toothless grin, turned, walked away, and that

141

was it! All he wanted was for us to enjoy his village. He expected nothing in return.

The real surprise came when I asked the innkeeper about their employee who'd been so kind. They informed me that they had no employees to help with bags. This man was simply someone from the streets of the village who happened to be at the inn when we pulled up and offered to help.

Once again, the perfection of inner beauty shined through this man's "imperfections" and our judgments. He appeared as loving service, asking for nothing in return. This time, however, the entire group had the opportunity to experience the gift from this angel in Tibet.

We all have a tendency to recognize the oddities of life from time to time, especially in others when they cross our paths. If we happen to see them while we're alone, we may simply glance, shrug our shoulders, and go on our way. If we're with other people, however, we may comment on what we see in order to ease our uncomfortable feelings about other people's curiosities. So while we may recognize the "imperfections," the question is, do we have a tendency to judge anything that's less than perfect as less than beautiful as well?

One day I was sitting at a stoplight in a rented car, in a big city where every make, model, and style of human that you could imagine was walking on the streets beside me. I was completely surrounded by people for the small eternity that I waited for the light to change. During that time, I had my own private review of life: all the new hairstyles, from '90s corporate to '60s retro; body art and piercing; business suits; briefcases; cell phones; and the latest skater apparel. Who could have asked for more diversity packed into one place? While everyone was interesting enough, there was one man who particularly caught my eye.

He had an obvious neuromuscular condition that made it difficult for him to control his arms and legs. He was dressed in a business suit, carrying a backpack, and looked as though he was on his way to, or from, an office. As he was waiting for the light, it appeared to be all he could do to keep his body in control and simply stand in one place. When the walk signal flickered, he, and the entire entourage surrounding him, crossed the street. I believe that there are no accidents in life, and I took the opportunity of his passing directly in front of me to look into this man's face. His mouth grimaced with the awkward and intentional effort that it took for him to complete each step. His eyes were focused and determined. It was *work* for him just to walk, and he was working hard!

As he disappeared into the crowd on the other side of the street, a feeling of gratitude came over me. I tried to imagine what it would have been like if he hadn't been there that day. When I did so, I missed him. I thought about what he'd brought to me in those few seconds, the courage that he'd demonstrated through his determination to be out in the world. I thought about how empty those moments of my life could have been if he hadn't been there. But he was. And through his very presence, that courageous man brought beauty to my day. I became a little teary eyed as I gave thanks for his presence and reflected, *How lucky I am to have seen this man today.*

I Invite You to Try This for Yourself

The next time you're in a public place, look into the crowd around you without being too obvious. Then make a mental note of one person—anyone. Ask yourself what it is about that person that touches you the deepest. Maybe it's their innocence or smile. As with the man that I saw from my rental car, maybe it will be something as simple as how this individual deals with life's challenges.

Now close your eyes and imagine what your day would be like if you didn't know that this person was in your world. Think of how empty that moment would have been, and how much you would miss him or her.

You may be surprised at the impact that such a simple exercise, in a brief moment, can make! Now you can give heartfelt gratitude and thanks for the person who was there for you, and what they taught you about yourself.

The Way We Choose to See

In addition to the beauty that's inspired by a sunset, a snowcapped mountain peak, or the work of a favorite artist, there are sources of beauty that come purely from the meaning that we give to our experience. In these instances, it's the way we see life that creates the *feeling of*

145

beauty within us. The experience of a human birth offers a perfect example.

Witnessing the emergence of a new life into this world by any account is a mystical and magical experience. Knowing what the outcome of a woman's labor will be, however, changes how we feel about what we see. For just one moment, however, if we could imagine ourselves coming to Earth from a world where the miracle of birth is an unfamiliar experience, witnessing the entire process could be disturbing, maybe even frightening!

Without the advance knowledge that "this is the way it is done on this earth," for all intents and purposes, as we witnessed the labor of new life, we would see many of the same signs that accompany the loss of life in our world. In a typical Western birth, we would begin by seeing a woman in obvious pain. Her face would show contortions intensifying in time with the labor. Blood and water would flow from her body.

How would we ever know that from the outward signs of pain that are often synonymous with death, a new life would emerge? It's all about the meaning that we give to our experience.

147

A Strange Beauty

The sky was on fire that night. The local radio station was dedicated to emergency programming, road closures, evacuation procedures, and hourly progress reports of the fires. For two days, and now two nights, the forests bordering the high desert mesa of northern central New Mexico had blazed with a fire so hot that it was creating its own internal winds, which were driving it ever closer to the oldest continuously inhabited pueblo in North America, the ancient Taos Pueblo.

As I came closer to town, a thick haze hung suspended in the hot, heavy air that had become trapped in the valley. Two days earlier, a single bolt of lightning from an afternoon thunderstorm had found its way to the dry brush and kindling of the forest floor. In a matter of moments, the mountainside above Taos was ablaze, and the fire was spreading at a dangerous pace toward the foothill settlements.

Although I knew that it was late afternoon, it was impossible to tell the time of day from the eerie twilight that blanketed the area. From the safety of my vehicle, I couldn't take my eyes off the sight that commanded my attention from the road. The brightness of the flames cast an odd glow onto the low clouds, bathing everything below in intense and penetrating hues of red, pink, and orange. As I looked at the backs of my hands, still holding on to the steering wheel, I realized that the colors in the sky were so deep and rich that even the bluish cast of my veins had taken on the rich colors of the glow.

Immersed in the experience, for just an instant, I *felt what I was seeing* without thinking of the devastating consequences that would surely result as the fire swept across the mountainside. I gazed at the strange beauty of the fires and marveled, *These are the kind of colors that artists have tried for centuries to capture on canvas, and here they are painted across the sky in a way that could never be reproduced by a human. How beautiful . . . how absolutely beautiful!*

149

Suddenly, the tone of the announcer's voice on the radio shifted from the calm of providing information to the urgency of reporting a new development. "The winds have changed," I heard him say, "and the fire may burn in one of two directions. Either it will continue to burn up the valley toward the homes on the other side of the mountain, or it will come our way, toward the town of Taos. We're advising people on the eastern edge of town to be ready for evacuation."

The eastern edge of town?! That's where I am right now! In that moment, the fire immediately looked very different to me.

In the time that it takes to hear a single sentence, the fire went from being an object of awe and beauty to a threat, as I realized that it now jeopardized the lives of people, horses, cattle, and other animals in its path. It was absolutely terrifying! I began to think about all of the wildlife that frequently gets trapped in fires that burn so quickly. There are always stories of charred corpses of deer, elk, and smaller forest dwellers that become disoriented by the chaos from the roar of flames, hot winds, heat, and smoke, and lose their way. There are also stories of firefighters, who, while risking themselves to save the lives and property of others, suddenly become surrounded by flames as a fire unexpectedly changes course and closes off their exit routes.

I share this story for a reason beyond simply honoring the memory of all who worked so hard to contain the Taos Pueblo fire of 2003.[2] For me, this fire reinforced a principle that many ancient and indigenous traditions have held sacred for centuries. During the time that I watched the flames, the fire itself did not change. It was still the same fire that it had been moments before, burning hot, wild, and free. *What had changed was me.* Specifically, I changed the way that I felt about the fire. In one moment, I saw the flames as a source of fascination and strange beauty. Only seconds later, the same flames became the source of anxiety, and in all honesty, not a small degree of fear! If I hadn't known that the flames leaping into the sky above the treetops threatened homes and life, in all probability they would have remained a thing of beauty. The realization, however, changed the way I felt about what I was seeing.

151

Many people reported having a similar experience as they watched the televised images of the Challenger space shuttle disaster over eastern Florida in 1986. Until they knew what they were seeing that day, spectators saw the billowing white clouds over Cape Canaveral contrasting against the deep blue backdrop of the south Florida sky as a beautiful spectacle of awe-inspiring technology. Once they knew that something had gone horribly wrong, however, and that the lives of the entire crew had been lost, the puffy white clouds lost their beauty and became the lasting symbol of a nation's pain and loss.

The principle is simply this: Although we may not have the power to determine *what* happens in every moment, we do have the power to determine our feelings *about* what happens. In this way we're given the key to change even the most hurtful experiences into life-affirming wisdom that becomes the foundation of our healing. Within the space of a few brief seconds, while I watched that fire in Taos, I had changed my experience simply through the way I felt about it.

152

The Power of Beauty

Recent discoveries in Western science now add to a growing body of evidence suggesting that beauty is a transformative power. More than simply an adjective that describes the colors of a sunset or a rainbow following a late-summer storm, beauty is an experience— specifically, *beauty is our experience*. Humans are believed to be the only species of life on Earth with the capability of perceiving beauty in the world around them, and within the experiences of their lives. Through our experience of beauty, we're given the power to change the feelings that we have in our bodies. Our feelings, in turn, are directly linked to the world beyond our bodies.

The ancients believed that feeling—*especially the form of feeling that we call "prayer"*—is the single most powerful force in the universe. As we've discussed, feeling and prayer do, in fact, directly influence the physical matter of our world. So when we say that beauty has the power to change our lives, it's no exaggeration to say that the same beauty also has the power to change our world!

The key is that we must find a way to see beyond the hurt, suffering, and pain that the world is showing us and recognize the beauty that already exists in all things. Only then will we have unleashed the potential of prayer in our lives, and its power in our lives.

Finding Beauty Where Others Find None

To help us in our quest to make sense of things, we're shown living examples by the great masters of today, as well as of our past. Several years ago the world lost one such master: Mother Teresa. "Mother," as those close to this great woman would call her, would shuffle down the streets near her home in Calcutta, India, and find beauty where few people believed that beauty could exist. Amidst the filth of garbage and debris in the gutters, the stench and the decay of rotting food and unidentifiable carcasses in the alleys, she would notice a mass of cow dung in the street. Growing in the dung she would find a flower. In that flower she would find life, and in that life she found beauty in the streets of the city.

With no words of explanation, no rationalization, and no justification, masters such as Mother Teresa believe that beauty simply exists. It is already here. It is everywhere and always present. Our role is to find that beauty. Life is our opportunity to seek it out and to allow the beauty that we discover in all things—from the deepest hurts to the greatest joys—to become the standard to which we hold our lives and ourselves.

Through her sheer will and determination, Mother Teresa applied the simple elegance of

154

her beliefs to life, and forever changed the ancient stigma attached to the so-called untouchables, the diseased and dying people of India's streets. Without judging them as "less than" anyone else, she and her Sisters of Charity volunteers would go out each day to search for the people they called "God's children." Historically shunned by Indian society, and sometimes even their own families, the sisters would take these people to the hospices that they created to give them dignity and privacy in their last remaining hours on Earth.

The sisters continue their mission to this day. I've made it a point to visit their facilities in the past and found the women performing a noble service that few people have the willingness or emotional strength to duplicate. They are truly angels that walk in this world. I think of the sisters and Mother Teresa often, and know that if they can find beauty in the streets of Calcutta, then I can recognize the beauty that exists anywhere I may find myself.

This is the power of beauty. The application is clear; the instructions are precise. The beauty that we experience in our lives is the blueprint for what is reflected in our world. In our high-tech era of miniaturized circuits and computerized devices to boil our water, it may be easy to overlook the power that beauty offers in our lives. Within the quantum understanding of a world where our inner beliefs become our outer world, what technology could be simpler, or more powerful?

Chapter Five

THE FIFTH SECRET:
CREATING YOUR OWN PRAYERS

*On a day when the wind is perfect,
the sail just needs to open and the world
is full of beauty. Today is such a day.*

— Rumi

PRAYER IS THE LANGUAGE OF GOD AND THE
ANGELS. FROM THE WISDOM RECORDED IN THE
DEAD SEA SCROLLS TO THE NATIVE PRACTICES
THAT HAVE SURVIVED UNTIL THIS DAY, PRAYER IS
UNIVERSALLY DESCRIBED AS A MYSTICAL LANGUAGE
WITH THE POWER TO CHANGE OUR BODIES, OUR

lives, and the world. Within these same traditions, however, there are many different ideas
regarding the most effective ways to "speak"
the language of prayer. In its own way, each
spiritual practice throughout the ages has put
its unique spin on precisely what prayer is,
how it works, and how to apply it in our lives.
Ultimately, what we find is that the language
of prayer has no rules, and cannot be done in
a right or wrong manner. It lives within us as
something that comes naturally: feeling.

In his description of feeling as prayer,
the abbot in Tibet clearly stated this timeless

wisdom that was lost to the West long ago:
"When you see us chanting for many hours
a day, and when you see us using the bells,
bowls, chimes, and incense, you're seeing
what we do to create the feeling in our body.
Feeling is the prayer!" Immediately following
his explanation, he then returned the question
to me, asking, "How do you do this in your
culture?"

It's strange how a single question, asked
in just the right way at just the right time,
can crystallize a belief that we may have had
trouble putting words to in the past. As I heard
the abbot's question, I had to reach deep inside

of myself to explain how I believed Western prayers work. In that moment, I began to realize the full impact of early biblical edits.

When the books that preserved the wisdom of emotion and feeling disappeared from our traditions, we were left on our own to understand feeling and prayer to the best of our ability. Today, 17 centuries later, we find ourselves living in a culture where we discount our feelings, deny them, or sometimes just ignore them completely. This has been especially true for men in our society, although this tendency is changing. It's as if we've been operating the cosmic computer of consciousness and feeling for almost 1,700 years with no operating manual. Eventually, even the priests and people of authority began to forget the power of feeling in prayer. It was then that we started to believe that our words are the prayers.

If you ask someone on any street, or in any airport or shopping mall, to describe prayer, more often than not they'll recite the *words* of familiar prayers to answer you. When we say things like "Now I lay me down to sleep," "God is great, God is good," and "Our Father, who art in heaven," the belief is that we're saying a prayer. Could the words be a "code"? Rather than being the prayer itself, could the words that remain today be the formula that someone else designed long ago to create the *feeling* of the prayer within us. If so, then the implications are vast.

We are always feeling in each moment of every day of our lives. While we may not always be aware of just *what* we're feeling, we are feeling nonetheless. If feeling is the prayer and we're always feeling, then that means we're always in a state of prayer. Each moment is a prayer. Life is a prayer! We're always sending a message to the mirror of creation, signaling healing or disease, peace or war, honoring or dishonoring our relationships with those we love. "Life" is the Mind of God sending back to us what we feel—what we've prayed.

When Prayers Stop Working

During the 1972 studies documenting the effects of meditation and prayer in different communities (discussed earlier in this book), the results were clearly shown to be more than coincidence or a fluke. The experiments

162

were subject to all of the scrutiny that would accompany any other reliable scientific study in a controlled laboratory environment. The effects were real. And they were documented.

During what researchers called the "window"—the time when people trained in the techniques felt "peace" within their bodies— the world around them reflected that peace. The studies clearly show that there were statistically significant declines in the key indicators that the researchers were observing. As I mentioned before, traffic accidents, visits to the emergency room, and violent crimes all diminished in number. In the presence of peace, all that could happen was peace. As interesting as these results are, however, what they show next has been an ongoing mystery to those studying the findings.

When the experiments stopped, the violence was renewed, in some instances reaching levels even greater than before the experiments began. What happened? Why did the effects of the meditations and prayers appear to stop? The answer to this question may be the key to understanding the power of our lost mode of prayer. What happened was that the trainees *stopped* what they were doing. They stopped

163

their meditations. They stopped their prayers. And this is the answer to our mystery.

In large part, the studies reflect the way that we've been taught to meditate and pray in our lives today. On a typical day, we go about the routines of our lives as businesspeople, students, and parents just doing the things we do. At a certain time of the day, we set a little "spiritual time" aside. Maybe we close the door for some privacy at the end of the day, after the dishes are done, the kids are in bed, and the laundry is finished. We light candles, turn on some inspirational music, and offer prayers of thanks or enter into meditations of peace. Then, when we're finished, we *stop* what we're doing. We leave our sanctuary and return to the "real" world. While I may have exaggerated some things here, the idea is that our meditations and prayers are often something that we *do* at some point in our day, and when we're finished, *we stop*.

If we believe that prayer is something that we *do*, then it makes perfect sense that when the prayer stops, the effect of the prayer stops as well. Prayer is a short-lived experience if we assume that our prayers are the gestures of our open hands placed palms together in front of our hearts and the words that we speak during that time. Between the ancient texts recovered in the 20th century, the native prayer of rain, and the story of the abbot in Tibet, however, we know that prayer is more than what we *do.* Prayer is what we *are!*

Rather than something that we *do* sometimes, these traditions invite us to accept prayer as something that we *become* always. While it's impossible to kneel in prayer 24 hours a day and recite the words that the ancients left for us until we can recite them no more, it's not necessary to do these things to be in prayer. Feeling is the prayer, and we feel all of the time. We can feel our gratitude for the peace in our world because there is always peace somewhere. We can feel the appreciation for the healing in our loved ones, as well as ourselves, because we are healed and renewed to some degree every day.

The reason that the effects of the experiments seemed to come undone is because the prayers ended. The peace that was held in place by the "beautiful and wild force" within the people who prayed and meditated simply dissolved when the means to hold it in place stopped. This may be precisely what the

165

Essenes were trying to convey to the people of their future through the language that they left for us more than 2,000 years ago.

Recent translations of ancient manuscripts in Aramaic, the language of the Essenes, offer new insights into why the records of prayer may appear to be so vague. By retranslating from the original documents, it becomes obvious that tremendous liberties were taken throughout the centuries with the wording and intent of the ancient authors. While attempting to condense and simplify the intended ideas, as the saying goes, a lot was lost in the translation.

With regard to the power of prayer, a comparison of the modern biblical version of "Ask and you shall receive," for example, with its original text gives us an idea of just how much can be lost! The modern and condensed passage in the King James Version of the Bible reads:

> "Whatsoever ye ask the Father in my name, he will give it to you. Hitherto have ye asked nothing in my name: Ask and ye shall receive, that your joy may be full."[1]

When we compare this to the original text, we see the key that is missing:

"All things that you ask straightly, directly . . . from inside my name, you will be given.
So far you have not done this. *Ask without hidden motive and be surrounded by your answer.*
<u>*Be enveloped*</u> *by what you desire, that your gladness be full.*"[2] [Author's emphasis]

In these words, we're reminded of the quantum principle that tells us that prayer is consciousness. It's a state of being that we're in, rather than something that we do at a certain time of day. By inviting us to *be surrounded* by our answer and *be enveloped* by what we desire, this passage reminds us in words of precisely what the abbot and my friend David showed us in the shared wisdom of their traditions. We must first have the *feeling* of our prayers answered in our hearts *before* they become the reality of our lives.

In the passages above, Jesus suggests that those he's speaking with haven't done that. While they may *believe* that they asked for their prayers to be answered, if their asking was simply the words "Please let these things

168

happen," then he says that this isn't a language Creation recognizes. He reminds his disciples that they must "speak" to the universe in a way that's meaningful.

When we feel as though we're surrounded by healed lives and healed relationships, and enveloped by peace in our world, that feeling is both the language and the prayer that opens the door to all possibilities.

Remembering Our Power

In the classic tale *The Wonderful Wizard of Oz*, it's only when Dorothy clicks her heels three times and says the words, "Take me home to Aunt Em!" that she's transported back to her family and loved ones. We all know that there's no "magic" per se in simply clicking our heels. If there were, we would see people appearing and disappearing from Starbucks lines and corporate boardrooms every time they did the same thing. Dorothy's words were not in the form of a request; they were a command. Who, or what, was she speaking to?

The command was for her! She wasn't instructing the good witch Glinda or the

Munchkins around her to perform an act of magic. Dorothy was the one with the slippers that became "power objects" in her journey. Just as a shaman's stone, Moses' staff, or Joseph's coat provided a focus for the power within their owners, Dorothy's shoes did the same for her. The three clicks were the trigger within Dorothy for her to *feel* the feeling as if she were home—and in a heartbeat, she was!

There's almost a universal sense that we have ancient and magical powers within us. From the time we're children, we fantasize about our ability to do things that are beyond the realm of reason and logic. And why not? While we're children, the rules that say miracles can't happen in our lives have not yet been ingrained in us to the point that they become limits in our beliefs.

Is it possible that our sense of connecting with a greater force is so universal, and that we so long for this connection, that we've preserved the ancient formulas to do so, while forgetting how to use them in our lives? Could our memories of fairy tales and magic, for example, have preserved keys to our lost mode of prayer without our even realizing it? If feeling is the prayer, then the answer to these questions is a great big *yes!* With this possibility in mind, let's examine some familiar examples of how the code for prayer has been handed down through the ages.

Perhaps the best-known and most universal prayer in the world is the Lord's Prayer. Its words are honored by nearly one-third of the world's population, the two billion Christians who look to the words of this ancient code for comfort and guidance. While the entire prayer is often recited in religious services, the first two lines are known as the Great Prayer: "Our Father who art in heaven, hallowed be thy name."

171

Rather than simply reciting the familiar words, I invite you to try an experiment. As you read the words of the Great Prayer, or perhaps say them out loud, make a mental note of how the words make you *feel*. How do you feel as you personally speak to the force that created the entire universe, as well as the life in each cell of your body? What do you feel as you acknowledge that the name of God is a holy name to be used only in an honoring and sacred way? There are no right or wrong ways to feel about this prayer. The point here is that the words that were recorded more than

2,000 years ago were designed to elicit feeling! Unbound by time and civilizations, the words speak to the part of us that's constant: our hearts. Whatever feeling the words create in you, that feeling is *your* Great Prayer.

The 23rd Psalm is a code that works in the same way. Although typically used as a prayer of comfort during times of need, such as the passing of a loved one, this powerful code is designed to create that peace within the living. Beginning with the very first line: "The Lord is my shepherd, I shall not want," we begin to feel as though we're watched and cared for in this world. Although the precise translations vary, the word *shepherd* is a constant in all of them. It's clear that this word was used intentionally because of its powerful metaphor, and the sense of being cared for that it conjures within us.

Perhaps one of the most amazing codes of comfort is recorded as having been given to this world by God for the purpose of blessing and peace. It is this ancient benediction that was discovered in 1979, inscribed on two tiny strips of silver shaped like a scroll. This passage from the book of Deuteronomy 6:22–26, is dated to 400 years *before* the Dead Sea Scrolls, and is believed to be "the earliest biblical passage ever found in ancient artifacts."[3] In the three phrases of the code, God prescribes a blessing for Moses to share with his people. In his ancient instructions, God told Moses, "This is how you must bless the Israelites." Following his precise instruction as to how the prayer is to be used, he offered the code to Moses as follows:

> May Yahweh bless you and keep you.
>
> May Yahweh let his face shine on you and be gracious to you.
>
> May Yahweh show you his face and bring you peace.[4]

He completes his instruction to Moses by saying, "This is how you must call down my name . . . and then I shall bless them." In this way, the prayer itself was preserved through the words that make us feel these things.

Putting It All Together

It's probably obvious by now that the central theme of this chapter is that feeling is the prayer! Embracing this principle, we're

given the great secret to having every prayer answered without fail. The key is that we must *become* the very things that we choose to experience in our lives. If we're looking for love, compassion, understanding, and nurturing in our lives, we must develop those very qualities within ourselves so that the Mind of God can mirror them back to us in our relationships. If we want abundance, we must feel gratitude for the abundance that already exists in our lives.

Between knowing this, and knowing of the hidden power in beauty, blessing, wisdom, and hurt, how do we put these things to work in our lives? What do we do with these ancient secrets to get through the tough times in life? Probably the best way to answer this question is simply to apply these keys in an example.

Earlier, I used the story of Gerald to show how we sometimes find ourselves drawn into the situations that bring us our deepest hurt, under circumstances that we least expect, and in times that we least expect it. In Gerald's case, he had lost everything that he loved: his wife, his children, his home, and his friends. Even his own parents had temporarily disowned him in response to the pain that he caused in their lives. By simply making choices that he felt he had to make, the ripple effect had led him directly into a Dark Night of the Soul.

Once he found himself in his Dark Night, Gerald had a choice. He could either let himself slip ever deeper into the dark spiral of anger, sadness, betrayal, and despondency that's typical of traumatic loss. Or, he could reach deeply into his soul for the strength to make sense of what had happened and pull himself out, knowing that he would be a better man afterward. While it definitely takes strength to get through such times in life, strength alone isn't enough. We cannot transcend a Dark Night experience by using our strength to beat it into submission! We must have something to put our strength into—a process. For Gerald, the following was the way he began his process.

— **Hurt Is the Teacher, Wisdom Is the Lesson:** The key to healing whatever tests life brings to us is that we can hurt only when we're ready to hurt. That is, only when we already have all of the emotional tools to heal our pain can we draw to us the experiences to demonstrate our mastery. This is the subtle yet powerful secret to coping with suffering.

The only way that Gerald could have created what he described as the "mess" that he found himself in was to have the building blocks of understanding that gave his life changes meaning. Simply knowing this gave Gerald hope, a new way to look at his life, and the strength to move through his process, rather than giving up. The blessing was the place for him to apply his strength.

— **Blessing Is the Emotional Lubricant:** When we apply the steps of the blessing process described earlier, we suspend our hurt long enough to replace it with something else. In Gerald's case, I invited him to bless everything about his experience. "Everything?" he asked.

"Everything!" I replied. The key to the success of blessing is that it acknowledges everything from the one who hurts, to the one who is hurting.

Gerald began by blessing himself—after all, he was the one who was hurt. Then he blessed the woman who betrayed him. He believed that she was the source of his hurt. He completed his process by blessing all those who had witnessed the hurt. This included

177

his daughters, his wife, his parents, and his friends. In the blessing, he suspended his own hurt long enough to let in something else. That "something" was the ability to see the big picture and make sense of the seemingly senseless things that were happening in his life. Through the new meaning of his life experience, he found beauty in the process.

— **Beauty Is the Transformer of Our Hurt:** Beyond something that we see only with our eyes, when we can see the symmetry, balance, and the give-and-take of a situation, we begin to see why things have happened the way they have. This is where the magic occurs! When our hurt makes sense to us and we can see the light at the end of the tunnel, we begin to feel differently about our experience. In that difference, our hurt becomes wisdom. This is where the healing begins.

— **Feeling Is the Prayer:** Ancient traditions remind us that the world around us is nothing more and nothing less than the mirror of what we've become in our lives: what we feel about our relationships with ourselves, one another, and, ultimately, God. Scientific evidence now suggests precisely the same thing; what we feel inside our bodies is carried into the world beyond our bodies.

For Gerald, as well as for many of us, this is a new, and very different, way of seeing things than we were taught growing up. It is also empowering. Within days of beginning his process, Gerald was able to bless and redefine his hurt and bitterness. His new feelings became the prayer that he sent into the world around him. Almost immediately, his relationships began to reflect his prayers. While he still had to work at it, he and his ex-wife developed a healthy friendship. This was good for them, as well as for their daughters. Gerald also soon found himself in a new romance that mirrored his new view of himself. Together, he and his partner embarked on a journey of discovery that his former wife would have found threatening.

So in this way, Gerald healed his Dark Night of the Soul. I last saw him in San Francisco in 1990. He said, "Boy, am I glad that's over with. I don't think I could go through another one!"

"There may be more," I said. "Just because you come through one Dark Night doesn't mean that you'll never have another one. It just means that you'll be able to see it coming, and know beyond a shadow of a doubt that there's always a better life on the other side."

Creating Your Own Prayers

The foundation of everything that we're saying here is that the words of prayers themselves are not the prayers. While the words may be beautiful, ancient, and time-honored relics, they're simply the catalysts to unleash a force. And the force is within you! *You* is the operative word here. Just as the code in a computer sets a series of events into motion, our words trigger feeling in our bodies. But neither the code nor the words have any power until they're given meaning. For the code, it's the computer's operating system. For our words, it's our feelings.

Prayers are personal. The words that trigger a powerful feeling of gratitude or appreciation for me may not be as effective for you. So this is where you can have fun with prayers: Create your own! Find the special words that are meaningful to you, and you alone, to serve you as a sacred and secret prayer that's between you and God.

A prayer could be as simple as a single statement that whatever you're praying about is already accomplished. An example of this kind of prayer might be a simple phrase that you say to yourself each time you close the car door and turn on the ignition to go somewhere: "I give thanks for a safe journey and a safe return." While you state your prayer, feel the feeling of gratitude as if your journey were already complete.

To empower your prayer with the senses, you would see yourself doing something when you returned home, like taking the groceries out of the trunk and stacking canned goods in the cabinet or putting lettuce in the crisper. The key is that you can only take the groceries out of the car and put them away if you're back home. In this way, you've set the powerful intention of a safe journey by feeling as if it has already happened.

It's said that the Dalai Lama used such a prayer as he began the treacherous journey that led him from his home into exile across the rugged mountains that separate Tibet from

181

India. "I see a safe journey," he stated, if the accounts are accurate, "and a safe return."

If you are poetic, your prayers can reflect your creativity in the longer form of rhymes. Rhymes are both easy to remember and can become a part of your daily ritual. The important point is to give thanks for the feeling they create. I have a friend who offers this kind of prayer as he drives to work each day. His home and his job are separated by a mountain range, and an abundance of wildlife that often wander onto the road at both dawn and dusk are sometimes killed. Each time he begins his drive, his prayer begins as well: "All creatures great and small, safe today, one and all."

While it may sound too simple, I believe that the world works in this way: Creation responds to what we become—and to what we feel. Perhaps it's no coincidence that through the years that my friend has offered his All Creatures prayer, he's never had a mishap with the animals that dot the highway during his commute. While he often sees them off to the side of the road, or crossing just before or after he's passed a certain spot, his prayer has been answered every day.

I have another friend who does something similar each time she takes a business trip. Whether it's on a plane, in a taxi, or driving her car, she begins each trip by acknowledging the living intelligence that exists within even the things that we call inanimate objects. During takeoff in her plane, for example, she states: "This machine we've created from the dust of the earth, to serve us in life from the moment of birth."

Once again, while it sounds simple or even silly to some people, it is these words that create for her the feeling that she's in touch with the stuff that the plane is made of. In that sacred communion, she feels the empowerment of being connected with the machine that's responsible for her safety, rather than simply hoping for a lucky ride.

These are only a few examples. With the knowledge of how our prayers work, I invite you to create your own. Have fun with your prayer-poems. Share them with friends. Don't be surprised if you find that it comes very naturally for you to anchor and seal your prayers with a rhyme. We knew how to do this when we were children, and our children remember

183

how to do it today. Rather than being a silly thing to do, we may just discover that through such simple and joyful moments of life, we're using an ancient inner technology to access the most powerful force in the universe! And you thought it was just a simple poem.

Endnotes

Introduction

1. Rumi, Daniel Ladinsky, trans., *Love Poems from God, Twelve Sacred Voices from the East and West* (Penguin Compass 2002), p. 65.

2. These lines were taken from an interview with Bruce Hucko. Shonto Begay, "Shonto Begay," *Indian Artist*, vol. 3, no. 1 (Winter 1997), p. 52.

3. In 325 CE, Emperor Constantine of the Holy Roman Empire convened a council of the early Christian Church and asked for advice as to which books should be included, or canonized, into the form of the Bible that is still used today. The recommendation of the council was to remove 25 books, while editing and condensing another 20. Archaeological discoveries in the 20th century, such as those of the Dead Sea Scrolls and the Nag Hammadi Library, have given us insight into the contents of a number of these "lost" biblical books, some that had not been seen since the edits, in addition to original versions of at least another 19 books that were not included in the final version of the Bible, but which have been available in a modified form.

4. Edmond Bordeaux Szekely, ed. and trans., *The Essene Gospel of Peace, Book 2* (Matsqui, B.C., Canada: I.B.S. International, 1937), p. 31.

Chapter 1

1. Nobel Prize–winning physicist Max Planck shocked the world with this reference to the power of nature's unseen forces during a famous speech in Florence, Italy, in 1917. Clearly a man ahead of his time, Planck's insights were made nearly 80 years before quantum physicists demonstrated the existence of a unified field under laboratory conditions. John Davidson, *The Secret of the Creative Vacuum* (London, UK: C.W. Daniel Company, 1989).

2. James M. Robinson, ed., *The Nag Hammadi Library,* "The Gospel of Thomas," Claremont, California (HarperSanFrancisco, 1990), p. 137.

3. Colloquial prayers are informal prayers offered in everyday language. An example is: "Dear God, if just this one time I can get to the gas station before my gauge reads 'empty,' I promise I'll never let my tank get this low again!" Petitionary prayers are requests to God, such as: "Mighty God, I claim perfect healing now, and in all past, present, and future manifestations." Ritualistic prayers are perhaps most familiar. These are offered as specific words spoken at a specific time of day or year. Two examples are: "Now I lay me down to sleep . . ." and "God is great, God is good. . . ." Some people make a distinction between meditation and prayer,

viewing prayer as "speaking" to God and meditation as "listening" to God. During meditation, we're typically aware of a sacred presence that permeates our world and our being, and we apply the techniques of various teachings to experience what this presence means in our lives, as well as to harness it.

4. In 1887, the infamous Michelson-Morley experiment was performed to determine, once and for all, whether or not a mysterious substance does, in fact, bathe all of creation and connect the events of life. While the experiment was innovative, the results were subject to interpretation and controversy. An analogy of the experiment would be if we were to hold our finger above our heads to test for wind. If we concluded that because no wind was present, there was no air, this gives us a good idea of how the Michelson-Morley experiment was interpreted. Following this experiment, physicists concluded that the "ether" did not exist, and that something that happens in one place has no effect upon something in another part of the world. Now we know that this is simply not true. Michael Fowler, "The Michelson-Morley Experiment," U. Va. Physics Department (1996). Website: **http://galileo.phys. Virginia.edu/classes/109N/lectures/Michelson.html**

5. This powerful statement reminds us that the things we see in our world originate in another un-seen realm of creation. What we see as relationships, health, disease, peace, and war are merely shadows of what's happening in the higher realms that we call "dimensions" and that the ancients called "heaven." Szekely, *The Essene Gospel of Peace, Book 2*, p. 45.

6. David W. Orme-Johnson, Charles N. Alexander, John L. Davies, Howard M. Chandler, and Wallace E. Larimore, "International Peace Project in the Middle East," *The Journal of Conflict Resolution,* vol. 32, no. 4 (December 1988), p. 778.

Chapter 2

1. Rowan Williams, "As Eye See It: So Where Was God at Beslan?" *Virtue Online: the Voice for Global Orthodox Anglicanism* (Friday, September 8, 2004). Website: **www.virtueonline.org/portal/modules/news/article.php?storyid=1283**

2. James M. Robinson, ed., *The Nag Hammadi Library,* translated and introduced by members of the Coptic Gnostic Library Project of the Institute for Antiquity and Christianity, Claremont, California (San Francisco, CA: HarperSanFrancisco, 1990), p. 134.

3. "Aging Changes in Organs, Tissues, and Cells," *HealthCentral,* Website: **www.healthcentral.com/mhc/top/004012.cfm**.

4. "Chill Out: It Does the Heart Good," Duke University news release citing the technical study of the relationship between emotional response and heart health, originally published in the *Journal of Consulting and Clinical Psychology.* **http://Dukemednews.org/news/article.php?id=353**

5. Brigid McConville, "Learning to Forgive," Hoffman Quadrinity (2000). Website: **www.quadrinity.com**

Chapter 3

1. Williams, "As Eye See It."

2. Rumi, Coleman Barks, trans., *The Illuminated Rumi* (New York, Broadway Books, 1997), p. 98.

3. McConville, "Learning to Forgive."

4. Robinson, ed., *The Nag Hammadi Library,* p. 128.

5. Ibid., p. 129.

6. *Holy Bible, Revised Standard Version,* Luke 6:28 (Cleveland and New York: World Publishing, 1962), p. 60.

7. Ibid., Romans 12:14, p. 151.

Chapter 4

1. R. H. Charles, trans., *The Book of Enoch the Prophet* (Boston, MA: Weiser, 2003), p. 5.

2. Begay, "Shonto Begay," *Indian Artist,* vol. 3, no. 1 (Winter 1997), p. 52.

3. The wind actually split the fire in two that afternoon, so it burned in two separate directions. Fire crews contained both fires within days. Although the land was charred and fallen ashes made the water unfit to drink for a period of time, the Taos Pueblo itself sustained only minor damage.

Chapter 5

1. *Holy Bible, Authorized King James Version,* John 16:23–24 (Grand Rapids, MI: World Publishing, 1989), p. 80.

2. Neil Douglas-Klotz, trans., *Prayers of the Cosmos: Meditations on the Aramaic Words of Jesus* (San Francisco, CA: HarperSanFrancisco, 1994), pp. 86–87.

3. John Noble Wilford, "Solving a Riddle Written in Silver," *New York Times* (Tuesday, September 28, 2004), section F, p. 1.

4. *The New Jerusalem Bible, Standard Edition,* Numbers 6:22–27 (New York: Doubleday, 1998), p. 133. This version of the Bible has restored the original text that was modified or deleted during the 4th-century edits. Included in the restored text is the original and ancient name of God, YHVH, which was replaced in 6,800 locations of other versions of the Old Testament with words such as "Adoni," "The Lord" and "The Name."

Melissa Sherman

New York Times best-selling author **Gregg Braden** has been a featured guest for international conferences and media specials, exploring the role of spirituality in technology. A former senior computer systems designer (Martin Marietta Aerospace), computer geologist (Phillips Petroleum), and technical operations manager (Cisco Systems), Braden is now considered a leading authority on bridging the wisdom of our past with the science, medicine, and peace of our future. His journeys into the remote mountain villages, monasteries, and temples of times past, coupled with his background in the hard sciences, uniquely qualify him to bring the benefit of long-lost traditions to the forefront of our lives today.

From his groundbreaking books, *Awakening to Zero Point* and *Walking Between the Worlds*, to his pioneering work in *The Isaiah Effect*, Gregg has offered meaningful solutions to the unique challenges of our time. In *The God Code*, he ventured beyond the traditional boundaries of science and spirituality, revealing the words of an ancient language—and a timeless message of hope and possibility—encoded as the cells of all life.

Website: **www.greggbraden.net**

For further information, please contact Gregg's office at:

Wisdom Traditions
P.O. Box 5182
Santa Fe, New Mexico 87502
(505) 424-6892
ssawbraden@aol.com

Hay House Titles of Related Interest

YOU CAN HEAL YOUR LIFE, the movie,
starring Louise L. Hay & Friends
(available as a 1-DVD program and an expanded 2-DVD set)
Watch the trailer at: **www.LouiseHayMovie.com**

THE SHIFT, the movie,
starring Dr. Wayne W. Dyer
(available as a 1-DVD program and an expanded 2-DVD set)
Watch the trailer at: **www.DyerMovie.com**

Getting in the Gap, by Dr. Wayne W. Dyer
(book-with-CD)

The Jesus Code, by John Randolph Price

Prayer and the Five Stages of Healing,
by Ron Roth, Ph.D., with Peter Occhiogrosso

7 Paths to God, by Joan Z. Borysenko, Ph.D.

*Published by Princess Books; distributed by Hay House

All of the above are available at your
local bookstore, or may be ordered
through the Websites on the next page.

We hope you enjoyed this Hay House Lifestyles book. If you'd like to receive our online catalog featuring additional Hay House books and products, or if you'd like information about the Hay Foundation, please contact:

Hay House, Inc.
P.O. Box 5100
Carlsbad, CA 92018-5100

(760) 431-7695 or **(800) 654-5126**
(760) 431-6948 (fax) or **(800) 650-5115 (fax)**
www.hayhouse.com® • **www.hayfoundation.org**

Published and distributed in Australia by:
Hay House Australia Pty. Ltd. • 18/36 Ralph St. • Alexandria NSW 2015
Phone: 612-9669-4299 • *Fax:* 612-9669-4144 • www.hayhouse.com.au

Published and distributed in the United Kingdom by:
Hay House UK, Ltd., 292B Kensal Rd., London W10 5BE • *Phone:* 44-20-8962-1230 • *Fax:* 44-20-8962-1239 • www.hayhouse.co.uk

Published and distributed in the Republic of South Africa by:
Hay House SA (Pty), Ltd., P.O. Box 990, Witkoppen 2068 • *Phone/Fax:* 27-11-706-6612 • info@hayhouse.co.za • www.hayhouse.co.za

Published in India by: Hay House Publishers India,
Muskaan Complex, Plot No. 3, B-2, Vasant Kunj, New Delhi 110 070 •
Phone: 91-11-4176-1620 • *Fax:* 91-11-4176-1630 • www.hayhouse.co.in

Distributed in Canada by: Raincoast • 9050 Shaughnessy St., Vancouver, B.C.
V6P 6E5 • *Phone:* (604) 323-7100 • *Fax:* (604) 323-2600
www.raincoast.com

Take Your Soul on a Vacation

Visit **www.HealYourLife.com**® to regroup, recharge, and reconnect with your own magnificence. Featuring blogs, mind-body-spirit news, and life-changing wisdom from Louise Hay and friends**.**

Visit **www.HealYourLife.com** today!

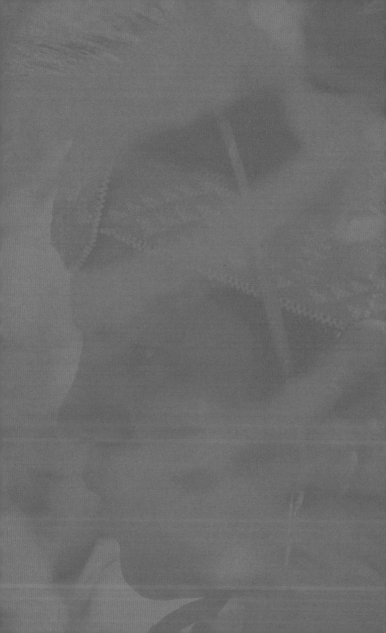